GW00645124

Sheila St. Clair was born in St. Austell, Cornwall, and moved to Northern Ireland in 1952. She has been writing, lecturing and broadcasting on the themes of folk culture, local history, and the paranormal since the mid 1950s. Sheila is a former chairman of the Belfast Psychical Society; and lists her hobbies as gardening, old houses, and reading history. She is married and lives in Lisburn, County Antrim.

UNEXPLAINED ENCOUNTERS

Exploring the Paranormal in Ulster

Sheila St.Clair

The White Row Press

UNEXPLAINED ENCOUNTERS

Exploring the Paranormal in Ulster

Sheila St.Clair

The White Row Press

First published 2001
by the White Row Press
135 Cumberland Road, Dundonald
Belfast BT16 2BB

www.whiterow.freeserve.co.uk

This book has received no financial assistance
from the Cultural Traditions Programme

Cover image: detail from Presentiment *by Carol Graham*
Cover design: White Space
Text illustration: William Clarke
Printed by the Guernsey Press Company Limited

A catalogue record for this book is available from the British Library

ISBN 1 870132 01 7

Contents

To all those who have walked with me
on this journey of discovery

Preface

The whole world knows that Ulster is a fairly paranormal place. What I hope this book will show is that it is a paranormal place in more ways than one. Properly paranormal, if you like. I hope to show that there is a discreet but pervasive paranormal background to life here, and that this background is a natural part of normal life.

In this book you will read of prophetic fires, 'human' mists, poltergeists, phantom limbs, a dancing table, a 'living' doll, numerous varieties of apparition, the bansidhe, disembodied spectral heads, 'possessed' houses, 'possessed' people, and much else besides, for Ulster is a veritable treasure house of paranormal experience and diversity. Most of the events described took place not in 'spooky' gothic mansions, but in perfectly ordinary places – roads, fields, hospitals and modern suburban houses. Most also took place within the last forty years or so. I have been either directly or indirectly involved with nearly all of them.

Every place, every society is in some way paranormally distinctive. In some communities, for instance, places rather than people tend to be 'haunted'. In Ulster I feel that the opposite is true. We tend to have a lot of poltergeistic and apparitional activity, more so perhaps than the rest of Ireland. We have very little mediumistic activity. One finds relatively few transport 'ghosts' here, whereas in Scotland there are quite a variety. We have few spectral ships. In all my years here I have only heard of two, which is nothing for a place with so much coastline

These phenomena have never really been systematically

researched. The Belfast Psychical Society which folded in 1970-71 is the nearest thing we have ever had to a semi-organised research group, and its interests tended to be mediumistic rather than paranormal.

The paranormal attracts few serious researchers in Ireland nowadays, and it attracts even less funding. It gets almost no institutional or academic support. No one likes sticking their necks out, and the forms of knowledge that I have been interested in gathering have always been considered to be a little beyond the pale. It is an amateur pursuit, and suffers for being so. I have had to get used to being a 'loner', and to steeling myself against prejudice and ridicule, if not downright abuse. Being seriously interested in psychic research has always been a little 'off'. Admit to actually doing it, and you were thought of as a little batty, and probably some sort of devil worshipper to boot. 'Thou shalt not suffer a witch to live', a caller to a local radio programme once told me. It was frightening to be the object of such feeling, even though I realised, belatedly, that it was misunderstanding and religious bias that spoke.

Happily, matters have improved. But what a pity it took so long! Over the last twenty years we have seen the growth of a more tolerant and educated appreciation of this particular field of research. The advance of academic parapsychology has also helped to make it 'respectable'. People increasingly realise that we maligned paranormal researchers might have something to offer. They accept that strange things happen, that we cannot pretend that they do not, and that it is legitimate to ask questions and seek explanations for them.

Another point I must stress is that this book is not about the supernatural. It is not about spiritualism, ouija boards, deep voice trances, or raising the dead. It is about the paranormal, by which I mean things that happen within natural laws but 'beyond the normal channels of sense'. The fact that they cannot be explained, does not make them any less real. At present 'we see in a glass darkly', but one day the laws that govern the behaviour of the – to us – bizarre phenomena detailed in the following pages will be widely known. What is now the terrain of parapsychologists and psychic researchers will one day be a branch of physics or biology and very probably taught in schools. Our pioneering efforts will seem hopelessly amateurish, and my successors in two or three hundred years, if it takes that long, will be out of a job!

The supernatural is different. It occurs outside of these undiscovered laws. As a Christian, I see the supernatural as matters which emanate from and are answerable to God alone. For me, it would be an impertinence to attempt explanations. The more widely this distinction is understood, the easier the work of future paranormalists will be.

For the taboos are still there. And we should not underestimate their power. One distressing theme that runs through this book is the the huge difficulty that a lot of people had in bringing their stories forward – in just telling another human being what had happened to them. I salute these people, for they have added much to our understanding of the paranormal in this little corner of the world.

Finally, I would like to thank everyone who helped in the preparation of this book: Pamela McAuley, Ian and Ruth Bailey, Barry Fitzpatrick, Eithne and Valerie, the staff of Laurel Hill Library in Lisburn, and David McCormick and Joan Morris from Larne. Thanks also to my long suffering husband Stanley Wyllie for his patient chauffeuring, map reading, consideration and support, and Peter Carr of White Row Press for his enthusiasm and editorial advice. Finally and most importantly, I would like to record my gratitude to the many friends and witnesses without whom this book could not have been written. My heartfelt thanks to you all.

Sheila St.Clair
August 2001

The Night Sister & the Doll

It is unsettling to experience a 'living' quality in something that in our everyday existence is inanimate. As human beings we expect some quality of 'normality' in what we see or hear, even when we are seeing or hearing it paranormally. When that expectation is upturned it can be very frightening, as this account, from a night sister coming off duty, illustrates.

The incident occurred in the grounds of a Belfast hospital. It is not a surprising location. Most hospitals have their store of strange happenings, and this is to be expected when one remembers how closely associated they are with birth, death, and almost every other stage of our existence. One could write an entire book on such sightings. Sister Rose McC, who had no prior experience of the paranormal, was privy however to an entirely unique manifestation. I was privileged to hear her account from her own lips.

'I had just taken up an appointment at Musgrave Park, working in the orthopaedic wing. After some weeks I found myself on night duty, and this took a bit of getting used to, as many things are accentuated at night, and the whole mood of the place is very different to the way things are in the daytime. I should say that I had been lucky enough to get accommodation in the nearby Nurses Home, and so in the morning when I got off duty, I could walk home in ten minutes or less.'

'The hospital was fairly new and stood in beautifully landscaped grounds, where you could sit out and relax when you were off duty. The walk home took me through the grounds.

'As I got closer I saw that the object was a very attractive doll...'

I travelled the same route every day and got to know it thoroughly.'

'On this route there was an oak memorial seat, presented to the hospital by the family of an erstwhile patient. On this particular morning, I was returning to my room at about six am. It was a lovely spring morning, and it was great to be stretching my legs, before going to bed to get some rest.'

'As I approached the seat, I could see an object propped up against the wooden arm rest at one end. As I got closer I saw that the object was a very attractive doll, in an elaborate Victorian costume, with a mass of golden curls peeping out from beneath a stylish bonnet. I smiled thinking that some little girl would be missing her dolly, and decided that the best thing to do would be to lift it and hand it in to lost property when I went back on duty.'

'With this intention in my mind, I walked towards the seat, thinking how fortunate it was that it hadn't rained during the night. Suddenly, to my complete amazement, the doll's eyes snapped open, and I found myself being regarded by a very cold, hostile gaze. I stopped in my tracks, more astonished than frightened. Then to my horror, very stiffly, the doll began to move. It slowly raised itself upright and leant against the wooden back of the seat. Then, never taking its eyes from my face, it began very slowly to 'walk' up the seat towards me.'

'I went cold all over, and found to my disbelief that I was like someone paralysed. I couldn't move a muscle, and my bag slipped from my fingers. Then mercifully I remember no more. A wave of nausea hit me, and I collapsed on the grass.'

'I was found by staff coming on duty. I was still unconscious and they rushed me to casualty thinking that I had been mugged. When I came round, at first I could remember very little, but as my head cleared, I asked the question that was burning a hole in my mind.'

'Did you find anything on the seat?' I whispered to my colleague.'

'She shook her head. "No. We found your handbag on the ground though, and the police said to tell them if there was anything missing.'

'There was nothing missing, of course. Not from my handbag. But the doll had vanished.'

'The shock I suffered kept me off work for several weeks. Every time I closed my eyes, I could see the hostile blue eyes staring into mine. The face of that doll was the most evil looking thing I've ever seen.' She looked tense and upset. I felt powerless to help.

When she had composed herself, she concluded her story.

'I checked with lost property several times over the following weeks, but no one had been in looking for a lost doll. No one.'

The sad thing is that the sister could not face going back to work in the hospital, and applied for another post. I must say, that when I thought about, I could hardly blame her. The incident was bizarre in the extreme, and I have never come across anything even vaguely like it in all my researching. I did, of course, ask certain questions of myself. Could she, after the continuous grind of a long period night duty, have experienced some kind of hallucination brought on by fatigue? I asked her if she had been on any medication prior to the event? She had not. So did she have some kind of clairvoyant episode? I wish I knew. One thing is for sure, I look at park benches very carefully indeed before I sit down!

The Naming of Parts

We don't like shocks and surprises. We tend to like things to meet our expectations. This also applies to our encounters with the paranormal. We assume that the things which are familiar to us will be reproduced whole in the world of the paranormal. But this is not always so. The reproduction may be partial. And this can be disconcerting. Individuals who can cope with the entire materialisation of an apparition of a phantom chair or table, go completely to pieces when faced with a partial materialisation, as in the case of W.B., a Tyrone farmer, who while walking up a country lane, was confronted by a phantom pair of corduroy trousers, tied at the waist with twine, and ending in hobnail boots, with no head, arms or torso above them!

Researchers love these partial sightings. You can theorise endlessly about them. One view is that they have something to do with the amount of energy available for materialisation, which is sometimes insufficient for the whole apparition to be seen. In other well documented cases the lower parts of the apparition may not be visible because the level of the road or floor that they are moving along has been raised in the years since they knew it, and the apparition, for instance a Roman soldier, is moving along the road as it was in his time. I have seen this once or twice, and it would appear to be quite a logical explanation. I am aware of at least a dozen instances of partial manifestations, but will recount just three.

The first appeared to a young journalist living in a flat on the Antrim Road in Belfast. David woke one morning to see a disembodied arm, a muscular, hairy arm in a rolled up shirt sleeve advancing towards him from the direction of the open bedroom door. To his astonishment, it continued to approach him, until it was within a foot or so of his face. It paused there briefly, and then vanished.

Alan immediately rang me, and described what he had seen with commendable professional detachment.

'I'm shaking yet,' he confessed. 'I can't believe that I saw it. But I did.' I tried to soothe his strained nerves. I told him that there was nothing to fear, and that it might never happen again. 'Can I have that in writing?' he asked.

Mercifully, that was the end of it. I puzzled over what he might have seen. If it was an hallucination it was an extremely vivid one, and my friend to my certain knowledge, had not taken any stimulant that might have produced one. I never tracked down the hand's owner, or arrived at any satisfactory explanation.

The second apparition was seen by a Tyrone farmer in his byre one afternoon, as he was mucking out his pigs. Out of the corner of his eye, he saw the shadowy form of a pig in the corner of the building. The pig was distinctly apparitional and consisted only of the head and forequarters. It vanished somewhere about the midriff. The startled farmer reacted instinctively, and lunged towards it with his grape. In the blink of an eye, the pig had gone. The farmer, who I think had to change his trousers after the incident, ran into the yard, and attempted to recover his cool.

It took him some time to recover from this experience, and a gargantuan effort of will to enable him to return to that outhouse. This was a most unusual sighting. But I wasn't completely surprised that it featured a pig. Pigs are magical animals in Celtic folklore; and in my experience they are the most common animals to manifest, after dogs. What had happened in this Tyrone byre? Had a reproachful porcine 'shade' returned to confront his executioner?

Our third account takes us from the hills of Tyrone, to the dreaming spires of Oxford. About five years ago, a Dromore lady, Mrs D went to that town to visit relatives. She stayed with her sister in a Victorian terrace house that belonged to one of the colleges. 'I had a lovely room at the back overlooking the garden,' she told me. On the second evening she retired early, exhausted after a day's sightseeing, and flopped down onto the bed. At this point in the conversation Mrs D unmistakably shuddered. I waited for her to compose herself.

'I'm sorry,' she apologised, 'but I can still see that 'thing'. After a few moments, she gathered herself and explained that, as she sat there, she saw a human head slowly emerge from the polished wood floor. It seemed altogether real. It was the head of a man with sallow skin and unkempt hair. Its eyes were open, and its mouth looked as though it might speak. In terror, she backed up towards the headboard. 'I could swear that its eyes were staring at me.'

'And then?' I prompted.

'And then it was gone,' she replied. 'It didn't fade, it was gone completely.'

She was too embarrassed to tell her host what had occurred. But the next night it happened again. After this second appearance the poor lady's nerves were completely shattered. She made some sort of excuse and returned home. When she got back, she told her daughter, who was understandably sceptical, and then she told me. Subsequent invitations to return to Oxford were met with ingenious refusals. She has not been back since.

I have known of only two local cases involving a disembodied head. One occurred in a farmhouse in County Derry, in almost identical circumstances. The other head appeared to a woman lodging in a large terrace house on the Antrim Road in Belfast in the late 1960s. She saw a female head with closed eyes rising through the centre of a rug near her bed. The head appeared to be that of a woman in middle age, and it disappeared after twenty or thirty seconds. As a devout coward, I must confess that I have no desire to have the personal experience that would make up the trilogy.

Haddock s Ghost

This is an account of a very unusual seventeenth century haunting. It is the story of a man who is said to have given evidence in a court of law five years after he died. It is recounted as set down by no less a figure than the Chaplain-in-Ordinary to King Charles II, who is believed to have had the account from the Reverend James Alcott, secretary to the Bishop of Down, who at that time was the famous divine, Jeremy Taylor. The incident has had ramifications that have continued to the present day.

I first learnt the strange tale of James Haddock from a clergyman acquaintance in County Down, who told me that he 'had James Haddock lying in his churchyard', and that he was known locally as 'the man whose grave never lay straight'.

I visited this curiosity with enthusiasm, having previously had only the vaguest knowledge of Haddock and his story, although between one thing and another, he and I were in time to become rather more personally acquainted! The rector led me into the older part of the churchyard at Drumbeg, and there before me, set flat on the ground, was a very worn grey stone, its lettering barely decipherable.

'You see,' he said. 'The stone lies crookedly and at variance with the tilt of any other stone in its vicinity, rather against gravity than with it.' This was true, for whereas other stones ran down towards the nearby path, Haddock's stone tilted away from it.

'It is said,' he continued, 'that Haddock in one of his many pronouncements prophesied that is stone would always lie crookedly as a symbol of the crooked dealings that he had suffered in life.' 'A number of sextons have attempted to right it, only to find it lying back at its original angle one or two days later,' he assured me. 'Now we just leave it alone.'

In the autumn of 1662, Francis Taverner, servant to Arthur Chichester, the earl of Donegall, was riding between Drumbo and Malone one evening when he was accosted near Drumbeg church by an apparition. Taverner vaguely recognised the apparition's features as those of James Haddock, whom he had known in life, and who so far as he knew, lay buried in the churchyard nearby. Terrified, Taverner and his companions spurred their horses and bolted. But the apparition caught up with them, and buttonholed Taverner, insisting that it wanted a favour.

Completely petrified by what they were seeing and hearing, Taverner and his colleagues fled again. This time they got away. But the apparition gave Taverner no peace. It appeared to him in all manner of places. It sang to him, or as the old manuscript puts it, 'pursued him with a most melodious twang', and threatened him with dire consequences if he did not take heed. Taverner took the threat so seriously that he was able to overcome his fear and listen. The spirit of Haddock was very clear about it wanted. It wanted a lawsuit taken against a man called Davis, the husband of Haddock's widow, claiming that the crooked Davis was robbing his son of his birthright.

Taverner found himself 'conversing' with the 'ghost'. He pointed out that he had no evidence, and that if he mentioned the apparition he would not be believed, and might even be accused of witchcraft. The spirit left, but Taverner could not keep what happened to himself. He confided in Chichester's chaplain, who advised him to consult the bishop himself.

So Taverner took the matter to the bishop. He immediately accepted the reality of the apparition, but was very little interested in its wishes. He had Taverner question the spirit about the afterlife, but Haddock was strangely unforthcoming. Appreciating that he would get nowhere with the spirit until its wishes had been dealt with, Taylor agreed to have the case heard in the church court in Carrickfergus, and have the accused man,

Davis, summoned to appear and answer the charges against him. Taverner was an unhappy party to this arrangement, for Davis was known to be a difficult and violent man, and Taverner was nearly as afraid of him as he was of Haddock.

A date for the hearing was set. On the day appointed, Davis' council immediately began to ridicule the testimony of Taverner's 'dead man'. Members of the public started to snigger. It began to look as though the case might be laughed out of court. Taverner, confused and nearly speechless, seemed completely overwhelmed by the occasion. When the judge, Bishop Taylor, asked him if he intended to produce any witnesses, in sheer desperation he cried out: 'Call James Haddock'.

The court fell silent as it waited to hear the bishop's reply. For a moment Taylor seemed steeped in thought, then he said:

'This man Haddock is assuredly known unto God, whose servant I am. Call James Haddock.'

Through the narrow windows, storm clouds were seen to gather. A rumble of thunder was heard. The usher rapped his staff of office on the flag-stoned floor, and cried out three times, 'Call James Haddock!' Lightening flashed, and to the court's astonishment, a man's hand appeared on the clerk's table, and a voice roared, 'Is this enough?' It most certainly was! The bishop ordered a thorough investigation into Haddock's son's affairs.

Taverner rode home. The vengeful Davis went after him, and matters would surely have gone ill if 'something' had not startled Davis' horse, causing it to rear up and throw its rider, who broke his neck. Five years later a man called Costlett, a crony of Davis, met with a similar mishap, outside the church at Drumbeg.

But that is not the end of the Haddock affair. In 1973 I received a very agitated phone call from an elderly resident of Drumbeg, who had gone to post a letter in the letterbox set in the churchyard wall.

'I was just posting it,' she said, 'when I saw the figure of a man in an old fashioned riding coat with an upturned collar. He appeared behind the churchyard wall, and from his movements I would guess he was on a horse.'

Sensibly, she didn't wait to see any more, but fled to her car,

*'I was just posting it, when I saw the figure of a man,
in an old fashioned riding coat...'*

letter still in hand. When she seemed calmer I asked cautiously
who she thought she had seen.

'That man Haddock,' she said, without any hesitation. 'He's
buried there, isn't he?'

Of course one could have argued for others, the list of
Haddock-related suspects being quite long. But thinking further,
I thought her guess was a good one. The next day I took myself
down to the churchyard, to look at the 'scene of the crime', but
both wall and grave were peaceful and deserted. Some ten years
later, I was recording a piece for UTV on the Haddock story,
when the director asked me to talk to the camera from in front
of the letterbox on the wall. I did so with what I hope was
professional nonchalance, but must admit to taking a cautious
look over my shoulder from time to time!

Signs & Portents

Tragic events are sometimes heralded by paranormal happenings. Occasionally, these are spectacular events like the White Light of Crum, the great ball of light that is said to roll over Lough Erne and has been credited with 'prophesying' both world wars.

More often, however, the paranormal event is an intimate, personal communication between two or maybe three people. This can happen a lot in wartime. Soldiers on active service are seen at home by someone dear to them, at the time of their death in battle. Many such manifestations have been reported. They tend to be fleeting. They are usually understood as 'farewells' or 'leave takings'. In behavioural terms, the experiences often seem crude or clumsy or incomplete. Which makes me think that we should see them as 'contacts' or bursts of energy, rather than pieces of behaviour. At these moments two conscious minds are involved in some kind of 'linkage'. And the minds do not need to be human. There is a case on record from near Moy in County Tyrone of a horse, a Clydesdale 'cross', sent to France during the First World War being 'seen' in his accustomed field at the farm, after he was killed at the front.

In most of the cases known to me, the sighting, though shocking at first, seems eventually to have brought a sense of consolation. Sightings can also occur when death comes close, as when someone is seriously wounded, or is involved in a traumatic event, such as a ship sinking. Warnings can also be communicated paranormally through so-called 'prophetic' dreams.

In 1954 I was in County Down cataloguing the folk beliefs of elderly people in the Mourne district, when I was directed to the cottage of an elderly woman, a maiden lady, who had an extensive knowledge of local folklore.

As we were chatting, I happened to mention that I was collecting information on apparitions. The old lady's face brightened.

'I have a story you might care to hear', she said.

'It's about a young soldier I knew who was killed at the Somme.'

The story she told me was the forerunner of several of the same ilk that I was to come across.

'We were neighbours,' she explained. 'His father owned the next farm to ours. Billy and I grew up together. Our farm was as familiar to him as his own.'

Her face grew sombre.

'Then the War came and Billy joined up to do his bit. His mother didn't like this for Billy was their only son.' There was a silence, and then she sighed.

'Little did I know that I would be the last one to see him.'

Then she explained how, one evening in July, she had been working in the kitchen when she saw a young man in uniform coming across the pasture. She recognised him at once, and joyfully flung the back door open and called out. She was surprised to see him for she had heard no word of Billy having leave. When she opened the door, to her surprise, there was no one there. It occurred to her that he must have gone round to the front of the house, though it wouldn't have been like him.

'We never used that door,' she told me. 'We always came in through the kitchen.'

She hurried back into the kitchen, and as she did so the heavy knocker on the front door gave a single loud rap. She ran up the hall and tugged the door open, but there was no one there, and with a shiver travelling over her whole body, she realised the truth of the matter.

I watched the colour in her face ebb away as she relived that moment all those years ago.

'I know who I saw,' she said. 'And I caught his expression. He looked so tired, and there was mud on his uniform. Yet for all that he looked glad to be home.'

As gently as I could, I asked her why she thought that he had come to her, and not gone next door to his mother? She thought for a moment.

'We had a kind of "understanding," she said shyly, 'and his mother was a nervous kind of woman. I dare say he wouldn't have wanted to startle her. So he came to me.'

There was another long pause, then,

'We got the news a few days later that our Billy had been killed when a trench that he was digging collapsed, and they couldn't pull him out. I dare say that's why the mud was on him, for he was always neat and tidy.'

Her eyes strayed to a faded photo on the mantelshelf, of a smiling, fair-haired boy in an old fashioned uniform ...

Of course these events do not only occur in time of war. Some years later in the County Down village of Loughbrickland, I heard a similar story about the son of the house who had been killed in a road accident.

'He was always so careful,' his mother told me sadly. 'But this time a car came round the corner on the wrong side of the road, and Ian couldn't dodge it.'

It seemed that Ian has gone to visit a relative in Banbridge, and had warned his parents that he might be late home, so when midnight struck and there was no Ian, they didn't worry unduly but prepared themselves for bed.

At about 12.15 am, his mother heard footsteps on the gravel leading up to the front door, and a long ring on the doorbell. Thinking her son had forgotten his key, the father went down a little grumpily and opened the door. To his astonishment there was no one on the doorstep. After taking a good look round, he returned to bed, muttering about the disturbance.

Then at about 2.00 am the feet were heard again, and again the bell rang. His mother rose this time and headed down the stairs to find two policemen on the doorstep. They came into the hall and with as much gentleness as they could muster, told her that Ian was dead, and that his body had been taken to the local mortuary.

The details they gave to the distraught parents were mercifully brief, of how a car had come out of a turning unexpectedly and their son could not avoid it. The father gave voice to one important question.

'So who rang the bell the first time?' he said over and over again. 'Who rang the bell?'

The mother said nothing. She already knew the answer.

Their experience was not unique. When no figure is seen these 'adieus' can take the form of a ring or a knock on the front door, which I always find very ironic, given the way these sounds are normally associated with arrival. I have also known of tapping on walls and furniture, and occasionally tapping on windows.

Why do these things take place? Are they attempts to warn those who wait? Or is it that, in the last moments of human consciousness, we have this overwhelming need to go 'home'? I don't know. But I do know that we should resist the temptation to see tappings as lesser or incomplete attempts at communication. They may perhaps be as much communication as the bereaved receiver can bear.

Another of these 'adieus' was experienced in Newtownards. In the 'mid 1980s' Mrs Kennedy was spending a few days there with her daughter and son-in-law, whom she visited regularly. The night before going home to Coleraine, she woke in the small hours to hear the breakfast table in the kitchen being laid in a rough, almost violent manner. Her daughter always laid the table before going to bed, but after a short while it became clear to Mrs Kennedy that this was not her daughter. The table layer then left the kitchen, ascended the stairs, and stopped outside her bedroom for a while before 'leaving'. Mrs Kennedy felt no fear. On the contrary, she was reassured by the presence and was able to go back to sleep without difficulty.

In the morning she discussed the experience with her relatives, who had heard nothing. On her return to Coleraine she was met off the train by her son with the sad news of the death during the night of a friend of fifty years standing. The friend had asked to be remembered to her shortly before her death. The lady had suffered from MS for many years. Her hands shook, hence the raucous crashing. Mrs Kennedy felt no surprise. No shock. When the bad news came she was ready.

Warnings can also come through dreams. In the 1960s I was approached by E.L., my son's godmother, a middle-aged, Belfast businesswoman and strict Presbyterian, who was not usually given to 'experiences' of any kind. She told me the following remarkable story:

'I don't dream a lot,' she said, 'but when I do I can usually recall it. And this dream was particularly vivid.' She looked troubled. It was obvious that it was going to be difficult for her to say what she had to say.

'I dreamed that I was standing on the bank of a fast flowing river, and that my sister-in-law was on the far bank. She was anxious to attract my attention, and when I looked across, she leaned over, and gestured me to hold out my arms. I went as close to the water as I could and did just that. Then she passed me a small baby, wrapped in a white shawl, and she said, "Look after him for me please." Then she climbed back up the bank and walked quickly away along a path. I took the baby, who was very, very young, and climbed back up the bank on my side of the river.'

She looked at me with eyes brimming with tears. 'I knew this meant something, and I really feared the worst, for my sister-in-law was heavily pregnant at the time. Five days later, she went into labour. There were complications. The surgeon saved the baby, but could not save her. Then I knew the meaning of my dream.'

I really felt for her, and had a lump in my throat at the thought of that young mother, who at some level knew what might be coming, trying to look after the little son she would leave behind.

The dream was lived out. Robert went to live with his aunt and uncle, and was reared as their own. I still see him sometimes as he goes about his business in the law courts in Belfast. His mother would have been very proud.

I am, I must confess, a prolific dreamer. On one never-to-be-forgotten occasion I dreamed the whole plot of a novel, from beginning to end. Unfortunately it only stayed with me long enough for me to be able to scribble down a few preliminary notes. So much for my blockbuster! Ah well…

Miles Apart

Paranormal events that communicate things across long distances make a deep impression on all who experience them. Here are two examples. The first communication took place between a house in County Antrim and another in West Sussex. These houses were the homes of two sisters. An interesting feature of the communication is that it did not take place along the 'blood line', but was received by the partner of the sister who was not involved. The second took place between Belfast and Canada. I don't think that the size of the distance makes any difference to the ability to perceive.

One winter's night in 1997, in a quiet Sussex seaside town, Mr and Mrs H went to bed full of apprehension. Outside, a storm was rising and all the indications were that it was going to be a bad one. The couple battened down everything in the garden that might be at risk. After placing torches to hand in case of emergency, they turned in, knowing that there was little chance of them getting much sleep.

Sleep proved impossible, so they decided to come downstairs and 'sit it out' with a consoling cup of tea - while the electric was still working. As the wife was putting on the kettle, a ferocious gust of wind blew the door off and threw it into the kitchen. It missed her by inches. At the same time the crash of glass and rending wood came from the sitting room. A palm tree had just burst through the window of the room in which the husband was sitting.

Although both were badly shaken, neither was hurt. However,

the house was at the mercy of the storm. Papers fluttered everywhere. Around them they could hear the crash of slates and ominous thuds and bangs as the houses nearby suffered. The telephone lines went down. Not far away, the side of a house was torn down and the bedrooms exposed to the elements. A caravan site was totally destroyed. Those who were relatively unscathed came to the aid of their stricken neighbours.

Meanwhile, back at Magheragall in County Antrim, the woman's sister and her husband were anxious. They had heard the late forecasts. They knew their loved ones would be in for a rough night, but they hoped that all would be well.

At about two o'clock in the morning, back in Magheragall, the brother-in-law of the woman in Sussex, was woken by a deafening noise. He was convinced that there had been an explosion in the house, maybe even a bomb.

He started out of bed. To his surprise, he noticed that his wife, a light sleeper, had not awoken. Shrugging on his dressing gown, the husband searched the bungalow for the source of the noise. Then he searched outside. Finding nothing amiss, he went back indoors. By this time his wife was also awake. He asked her about the 'explosion'.

'I didn't hear a thing,' she assured him. But the 'incident' worried both of them.

The next morning they rang the Sussex number, but got only a loud crackling on the line. The news bulletins were awash with reports of damage, injury and even death. Now thoroughly apprehensive and desperate for word of any kind, they rang another relative in England who was a fireman. He sketched out what might have happened.

Later that morning their relatives in Sussex rang them, and reassured them that no one had been hurt, but that the house had been quite badly damaged. The husband reported their lucky escape.

'Mary was in the kitchen when the door blew in. It's a miracle she wasn't hit.'

'When did it happen?' asked her brother-in-law in Northern Ireland.

'About 2.15,' he replied.

When he had put the phone down, the Ulsterman turned to his wife and told her what had happened. His face was pale.

'When I heard that almighty crash and nearly jumped out of my skin,' he said, 'I looked at the clock. It was twelve minutes past two. Now I know what I heard.'

His wife tried to be sensible.

'But you couldn't have heard their door blow off.'

The man shook his head.

'I know. But I definitely heard something.'

For those in the epicentre of this fearful and now famous storm, it was a night to remember. For the couple in County Antrim, the night was just as unforgettable, though for rather different reasons. The storm brought chaos and mayhem. Hundreds were injured. Hundreds more, like this Sussex couple, had phenomenally lucky escapes. Were others warned in the same way, that their loved ones were in danger? I would love to know, but don't expect I ever shall.

The second, rather chilling communication took place across a much longer distance. It was received by a colleague, Eddie R., who worked in the same further education college as myself, and discussed with me two days later.

Eddie's brother Don had recently moved to Canada on a two year business contract. He was, like Eddie, a bachelor, and the two brothers were each other's main family, their parents being dead. One evening Eddie was sitting watching television when the phone rang. The brothers had agreed to ring each other once a week, and thinking it might be Don, Eddie picked up the phone, to be greeted by static and heavy interference. After a moment he put the phone down, assuming that whoever it was would try to contact him again. The phone rang again almost immediately and he snatched it up. A barely audible voice uttered the words, 'Eddie, help me', then the line went completely dead.

Thoroughly alarmed, Eddie rang his brother's number, to receive no reply. He rang the overseas operator and asked if the incoming calls could be traced. But according to the operator there had been no calls. Eddie tried his brother's number again, without result. Then he tried his brother's boss, but again drew a blank.

The next day Don's boss rang him at the college to tell him that the previous day his brother had been hospitalised after a freak accident. When Eddie contacted the hospital he was told that Don had lapsed into a coma. After some weeks Don happily took a turn for the better. He came back to Ulster and his very relieved brother. Was it Don that Eddie heard on the phone? Eddie was quite adamant.

'It was Don, I know it. And who else would he want if he was in trouble but me?'

Knowing that a number of incidents of this kind are reported every year, I would have to admit, I can follow his logic.

The Flaming Cottage

Paranormal phenomena commonly reflect recognisable natural events, such as a high wind that suddenly blows up, a heavy mist, or a shower of bright sparks, such as might come from a bonfire. Fire or flames are seen quite often at the site of a psychic disturbance. One of the most famous phantom flames is that seen at Roslin Chapel in Lothian, Scotland. It is said to portend the death of the head of the St.Clare family. Sir Walter Scott immortalised it in his Lay of the Last Minstrel:

> *O'er Roslin all that dreary night*
> *A wondrous blaze was seen to gleam*

Single flames as from a candle are often quoted in relation to psychic phenomena, usually as a death portent. The colour of the flame is said to indicate the age of the victim, a white flame indicating a young child, and a blue flame a woman in childbirth. Larger flames usually have a more individual significance.

The following account has an intriguing prophetic component, and was authenticated by a number of witnesses known to each other.

In the summer of 1944 a group of young people took a weekend cottage in the Mourne mountains for a short holiday. They intended to do some walking and at least one of their number was a keen bird watcher. They knew the cottage quite well. It stood on the slope of a steep valley and was fairly remote. Some of them had stayed in it before, and had fallen in love with the bleak, rugged beauty of its surroundings.

The Saturday morning being fine, the small group had set off early to walk down to the head of the valley, and to return along the other side, from which their cottage, being one of half a dozen or so dwellings well spaced along the valley sides, would be clearly visible to them.

Some time around 3.00 pm, after their picnic lunch, they were striding back in good order on the far side (which boasted a good 'B' road), when one of the party stopped abruptly, and pointed across the valley to where their cottage could be clearly seen.

'Look! Look at the cottage.'

'My God. Its on fire!'

The group stopped and stared. Flames seemed to be erupting out of the building and its thatch was wreathed in smoke. They were at the farthest point of their walk. There was no way they could get back in time to save the cottage.

There was, however, another cottage only five minutes away, and they broke into a run.

'The fire brigade will never make it in time,' said Tom, the leader of the group, 'Maybe there's someone here who could drive us over?' It was a faint hope, but their only one. Their luck was in, and the woman of the house, taking one horrified glance out of the door, ran for the telephone and called the fire brigade. After that, she and the distressed walkers piled on board the elderly vehicle that stood in the yard, and headed for the burning cottage.

It took all of twenty-five minutes to skirt the head of the valley and get back to the road on the opposite side, where the cottage stood. As they rounded the last bend before the cottage, they were mystified to note that there was no smell of burning or sign of smoke.

Then the cottage itself came into view and the mystery deepened. Not only was the cottage not on fire, but there was no sign of it ever having been so. It was just as they had left it that morning. Entirely intact.

Tom broke the silence.

'I know what I saw,' he declared. 'I saw flames shooting out of the windows and door, and the smoke haze over the thatch.'

Somewhat edgily, the others agreed with him, as did the woman who had come to their aid. At that moment they heard the distant sound of the fire engine approaching, alarm blaring. What on earth were they going to tell the firemen? In due course the fire engine rushed into view, to be greeted by five dishevelled, confused and apologetic people.

To cut a long story short, the fire fighters gave the place a thorough inspection. All was as it should be. Nothing seemed amiss.

Privately, the senior fire officer believed that the group had probably been misled by strong sunlight glancing off the windows. But what of the woman who had lived across the valley for most of her life? She seemed certain that she had seen a blaze. How could he explain that? He decided that she had been 'spooked' by the others. Carried along in the hysteria. Anyway, there was no harm done, so the firemen left, glad that there had been no need of their services.

The disturbed and chastened walkers had their supper and retired quietly to bed.

At about two o'clock in the morning, Elaine, one of the two women in the group, got up to go to the bathroom. At the top of the stairs she stopped and sniffed the air cautiously. There was a landing door at the top of the stairs as sometimes the cottage was co-let to two small groups, one downstairs, one up.

Cautiously, she opened the door. To her horror, she was met by flames and acrid smoke billowing up from downstairs. She had no time to wonder if this fire was real or imaginary. The heat seemed intense. The smoke nearly choked her. Slamming the door shut, she ran back and woke her sleeping companions. By the time they got back to the stairs, these too were well alight. The only escape route was out of a window and onto the flat roof of a shed. Getting out was an extremely hazardous operation. In the course of their escape Jean, the second girl in the party, missed her footing on the shed roof and fell to the ground, badly injuring her back.

The police, fire brigade and ambulance were called out, and this time there was work for the fire crew to do. As dawn streaked the sky the charred ruins of the cottage were a woeful sight to see. There had mercifully been no loss of life, although the group of walkers had lost nearly all of their belongings and seen their friend Jean carted off to hospital.

The fire officer told the police sergeant what had happened earlier in the day.

'Thank God the young woman who raised the alarm had been worried enough to sleep badly,' said the sergeant. The fireman nodded.

'Not many get a warning like that,' he said.

It was a weary and sober group who headed home for Belfast, with their heads full of an experience they could barely make sense of, and a tale that others would find hard to believe.

Fascinated by this story, I searched the record for similar experiences. Only one other account of a burning cottage came to light, an instance in the 1920s of a wildfowler outside Newry who came across a burning cottage in a wood. To his horror the cottage contained living people. At least it appeared to, until suddenly the cottage vanished, and the sportsman found himself alone in an empty forest glade, containing only the overgrown footings of a building, a cottage that had stood there in the previous century.

Local accounts tell of trouble between the militia and a group of 'ribbon men' in about 1835. The ribbon men, so called because they wore as their badge a twist of green ribbon, took refuge in the cottage. In the course of the skirmish, the thatch was set alight by musket fire. This had happened almost a hundred years before the wildfowler had seen the cottage. He was somewhat disconcerted to find that the surname of the locals was the same as his own.

The Baker & the Bansidhe

The bansidhe or 'fairy woman' is one of the oldest paranormal manifestations known in Ireland. Other Celtic nations know her by different names. In Wales they call her 'the dribbling hag' or y wrach y griva. In Scotland she is 'the washer at the ford'. Sometimes the bansidhe appears in the form of a bird, a flower or a bush. In Ireland, however, she usually takes the form of a beautiful young girl, and occasionally that of an old woman.

She has been known since before the dawn of history. Cuchulainn, 'the Hound of Ulster', heard her, as some centuries later did Brian Boru. And so far as we can tell she is still here, revealing herself in the time honoured way to the family and friends of the person she is 'calling'. The person called, however, will not hear her or know his fate.

Many years ago her origins were explained to me by an elderly man from the White Mountain area near Belfast, whose family had seen and heard their own bansidhe for generations:

> *'Just as individuals have their own guardian angels, the Creator also appointed a guardian to each family or clan. These celestial beings could not feel joy or sorrow, but when a member of their human family was approaching death, the good Lord permitted the angel to grieve. They were also permitted to warn the family and friends of the approaching tragedy …not all families had their own bansidhe, only certain ones that might be descended from High Kings …over the centuries by marriage and other means, a number of surnames were added to this list and it now numbers over seventy.'*

What we are saying, then, is that the bansidhe is a death messenger, and that her keening is intended to brace the family for what is to come. Like the biblical Rachael she is 'weeping for her children because they were not'.

In spite of its early royal associations, the phenomenon is relatively classless, and may be experienced by people in all walks of life. For the most part, the bansidhe was not seen but heard, as one witness told me, screeching 'like them oul' cats on the yard wall'. A succinct but hardly elegant description! I have heard the bansidhe on two occasions, and spoken to people who have heard her on three or four more. My family, which has Celtic Cornish origins, has a form of bansidhe known as 'the black birds', a group of crow-like birds which gather silently before the death of a family member. I saw them twice, and in 1962 my four year old son came running into the house saying, 'There are black birds in the garden and I don't like them.' He, of course, was completely unaware of their significance. They had gathered for my Auntie B, his great aunt Beatrice, who died shortly after.

The following experience, which took place at a west Belfast bakery, is one of the most memorable I have known.

In the early 1960s Tommy was a bread server with Hughes, then one of Belfast's best known bakeries. His day started at around 4.30 am, when he would collect his van and replenish it with stock, ready for the early run in the streets of the city.

This particular Wednesday morning things were a bit different, as shortly after Tommy clocked in for work, he received a phone call asking him to come home urgently, as his mother had suddenly collapsed and been rushed to hospital.

Shortly after Tommy had gone home, one of his mates came to the bakehouse door and said that something weird was happening in the yard beside the vans.

'I can hear someone crying,' he said.

Despite some good natured joking, he stuck to his story and eventually one or two of the other men followed him out to the vans. There they heard the distinct sound of someone in deep distress, and it seemed to be coming from the corner where Tommy parked his van.

*'One of his mates came to the bakehouse door and
said that something weird was happening...'*

Deeply uneasy, the men moved back to the bakehouse, and one or two of the older men discussed what they had heard in low, anxious voices. While they were speaking, the phone rang again, and the man who answered it was very white when he put the receiver down.

'Its Tommy,' he said. 'He won't be back in tonight. His mother died on her way to the hospital.'

One of the older men openly blessed himself.

'Now I know who was in the yard.'

'What name had Tommy's mother?'

Someone who lived close by thought it was McClusky. The older man went to the bakery door and listened. The weeping had stopped and the yard was calm and still.

'God be good to her,' he said soberly. 'For the bansidhe came for her.'

None of the other workers could make a reply, for they too had heard the bansidhe call.

The Radiant Boy

The following is an account of the appearance of an extremely rare phenomenon consisting of the apparition of a boy infused in a radiant, golden glow. He is naked and in the first flush of youth, and has been described as a 'luminous' spirit; silent but with very compelling eyes. He is known in Scandinavian literature, but appears very rarely in reports of the paranormal in Britain and Ireland. Like the bansidhe, he would seem to be a 'death messenger', who is given to visiting a particular person or family. However, he is a death messenger of a rather Faustian kind, in that those he visits will achieve great fame or prestige before meeting with a violent end.

Cathleen Crowe cites this story in The Night Side of Nature, *and reveals her source to have been a descendant of the family of the man it appeared to, whom she had no reason to doubt. I have never encountered this very singular manifestation, but think it is important to mention it to illustrate the breadth of paranormal experience that has, allegedly, been had here.*

In the late 1780s a young man called Robert Stewart was out shooting in County Londonderry. It seems that after a day's sport, he got lost and separated from his companions during a bout of heavy rain, and had to walk several miles looking for shelter.

At last he stumbled on a large house and knocked at the door to ask for directions. Its owner, a genial man whose name has not come down to us, recognised his visitor as a gentleman, and invited him in, explaining that Captain Stewart was welcome to stay the night, but as he had a house party quartered on him, the captain's accommodation would have to be rather rudimentary.

Tired and hungry, Stewart gratefully accepted the invitation, and was shown to a sparsely furnished bedchamber, which contained a bed hastily made up on the floor. He was heartened, however, by the fact that the room had a cheerful, blazing fire and an ample number of candles. Having been brought some supper, he soon fell asleep in his makeshift bed.

During the night he was suddenly awakened by a blaze of light and a feeling that he was no longer alone. To his astonishment, standing in the centre of the floor, he saw a beautiful boy, entirely naked, and bathed in a golden halo of light. For a long moment the captain stared at this apparition and was aware of a careful scrutiny of him by 'the boy'. Then, very slowly, the boy glided to the fireplace and vanished.

Once Stewart had recovered from his shock, he became extremely angry. Although he could not imagine how the trick had been played on him, he was nevertheless convinced that he had been the victim of a hoax.

Determined to take it up with his host in the morning, he crawled back into bed and once more fell asleep. The following morning, the young captain accosted his host somewhat icily, and informed him that he had not been at all amused by the prank. His host looked dismayed and summoned the butler who had shown him to his bedroom. The man looked very upset.

'If we hadn't had so many guests,' said the butler, 'I would not have put this gentleman in the boy's room'.

His master was angry,

'You know I have given strict instructions that the room is not to be used!' he retorted. He turned to Captain Stewart, 'If you come with me, I will explain.'

Somewhat mystified, the Captain followed his host into the library where he was told that this vision of a beautiful 'Radiant Boy', was a kind of death messenger in the family. He was reputedly seen every seven years, and whoever saw him would rise to fame and power and then meet with a tragic end.

Stewart was unruffled by this explanation. He told his host

that the chances of him rising to any eminence in the world were fairly marginal. Peace restored, he said his goodbyes, and left.

But Captain Stewart was wrong. Within a few short years he had become M.P. for County Down. In 1796 he inherited the title Viscount Castlereagh, and went on to achieve great fame in the field of politics, most notably as architect of the Act of Union between England and Ireland in 1801. By 1812 he had become British Foreign Secretary, consorting with men such as Wellington and Pitt. He was never popular and attracted many enemies. The family's Irish home was, of course, Mount Stewart, in County Down, now in the care of the National Trust.

In 1821 Robert Stewart succeeded his father to the title of Marquis of Londonderry, and was at the height of his fame, when tragedy struck. His mental health had been poor for some time. In the end his family was advised to put him under restraint at his Kent home. Alas, in spite of all the precautions taken to keep him from harm, he took his own life by cutting his throat with a small penknife, when all else was denied him. Thus did Robert Stewart fulfil the prophecy of 'the Radiant Boy'. The story of the boy was passed down through the Stewart family, but over time the name of the family that the boy was 'native to' was alas forgotten. This, then, is the only recorded appearance of this fatal apparition in Ireland.

By Water

Being near water can often render a location susceptible to paranormal events. The following incidents took place beside water and were, to coin a phrase, 'inextricably linked' to it. The first was given to me only months ago by Mr J.A.C., a retired civil servant, now working in the book trade. Though the incident took place sixty years ago, it made an indelible impression. I shall let him tell the story in his own words.

'In 1941, following the German air raids on Belfast, my father decided to evacuate the family to the country. Understandably many others had the same intention, which resulted in a shortage of rented accommodation in a number of areas.'

'At that time my eldest sister, recently married to a sergeant in the North Irish Horse and living in Ballykinler Camp, heard of a vacant cottage by Tyrella beach. For some unknown reason this had not been snapped up in the rush, and all the windows were covered by solid steel shutters.'

'We took the place for six months and moved down shortly afterwards. At the beginning the whole family (except my father, who could not leave his work in Belfast) stayed there, but after a few weeks without further air raids, the family moved back home – except for me and my brother Jack, who was three years my junior. It was coming on to summer and we pleaded successfully to be allowed to stay at Tyrella during the week, with the others coming down to join us at the weekends. At the age of sixteen I was confident that we could look after ourselves, and it turned out to be so.'

'The cottage lay at the end of the beach, about a quarter of a mile down its own lane from the main road, and very close to the sandhills. The only lighting was from oil lamps and candles. We had no wireless, and at night the only lights were the moon and the beam from the lighthouse on St. John's Point nearby. When it was misty, the mournful sound of its foghorn would carry across the bay, drowning out the lapping of the waves.'

'Although we were alone (except for the hundreds of rabbits in the sandhills) we felt no fear of any kind. Even when I first became aware that someone or something was watching me from the corner of the room I just accepted it and passed on to other things as though the person was an acquaintance. Only later did I find out that this someone was the presence of a young girl who had tragically drowned on a Sunday School excursion to the beach some years before. I learned that her body had been left in the partially built cottage overnight, as it was not till very late that it had been found in the headlights of the bus, pointing seawards.'

'On three occasions I was wakened at night to hear the clicking sound of one of our bicycles' pedals being reversed again and again. (The bikes were always brought in at night for security.) After listening for a minute, I would just drift off to sleep again, and think no more of it. Jack, my brother, fast asleep in another bedroom, heard nothing of what was going on and was adamant that he had not done it for a joke. Once again there was no sense of fear or even wonderment on my part about what had happened.'

'The most curious thing of all was the appearance on many mornings of a piece of wet seaweed on the front doorstep of the cottage. How on earth it managed to cross the twenty yards of grass separating the sandy beach from the doorway, I'll never know. With hindsight I feel that it was transported paranormally by the spirit of the friendly young girl, to let me know that she had lost her life in the sea. After that there were no further happenings, and I love to think that, knowing that she had 'told me' of her presence, the girl was then able to drift away to true happiness and peace in some other dimension.'

The second shoreside incident took place in North Antrim in the early 1970s. I was researching a BBC radio programme called Walk the Earth Unseen when I received a disturbing letter from Mrs MacV, who lived on the Woodstock Road in Belfast. She had had a slight heart attack, and to aid her convalescence she, her husband, and their son David, had moved to a holiday bungalow by the sea near Cushendall. The bungalow seemed perfect. It was close to the beach and though there was a road between them and the shore, there was so little traffic on it they were able to let their eight year old son come and go as he pleased without fearing for his safety. Because of her illness, she and her husband had a bedroom each. Mrs MacV was delighted with her room, which had a delightful view over the sea.

On her first night in the bungalow she went to bed early and was soon sound asleep. Waking suddenly about midnight, she was aware of the terrifying sensation of someone trying to climb over her into the bed. She fled the room. After some measure of calm had been restored, she spent the rest of the night in her husband's room. Her husband took her room, but received no sensation of anything, so after a few nights the woman moved back.

On her first night back, she again experienced the chilling sensation of someone climbing over her into the bed.

'I could tell it was a woman,' she told me, 'and that at one time the bed lay in the opposite direction, for she lay across me.' There were marks on the adjacent wall, which confirmed her suspicion that the bed had previously lain against it. She was unable to sleep there again, and the room was shut up.

Who was this woman? Discreet investigation revealed that the wife of the previous owner had drowned in a swimming accident. Her body had been recovered from the beach opposite the bungalow. The sorrowing widower had forsaken the bungalow and it had lain empty for over a year. They too had been a family of three with a son called David. Local people were reluctant to be drawn on the incident, and I sensed that there were contributory causes to the tragedy. Could this have been the woman clambering over Mrs MacV's bed?

I met Mrs MacV and heard the whole story. Mrs MacV was a sensitive and sympathetic woman, who was very receptive to 'atmospheres'. She talked about there being 'a sadness' in the house, which she felt very keenly. It was most obvious on the seaward side of the bungalow.

'I prayed for that woman,' she told me. 'I felt she needed help.'

Mrs MacV had also had the unnerving sensation that 'she was thinking someone else's thoughts'. This, coupled with the distressful atmosphere, disturbed her deeply.

Her son had also been drawn into the web. One morning, shortly after going off to play, he came running back into the house to ask his mummy what she wanted. His mother was confused.

'I didn't call you,' she told him.

'Mum, I heard you calling, "David, David," he replied.

'When?'

'Just now, as I was about to cross the road to the beach,' he answered.

The boy was sure he had been called, but Mrs MacV knew very well that she hadn't called him. This happened on three occasions. They later discovered that the previous owners had also had a son called David.

Who called David? Which David was she calling? And how was David MacV able to hear her? I think David heard 'her' because he had inherited some of his mother's psychic ability. Children have relatively good extra sensory perception. In our early years we have not yet been programmed, as most adults have, only to experience what it is proper to experience, and for that reason children may sometimes be nearer to the truth in such matters.

I recall as a very little girl, being punished for telling lies. I had told my nanny that I had seen Tiddles, the family cat, sitting on the rug in front of the nursery fire, licking himself and cleaning his whiskers. But how could I have? Tiddles had been run over by a van three days before, and I had attended his funeral in our garden. So I must have been mistaken, mustn't I?

Varieties of Lady

Are women more spiritually receptive than men? Are women more likely to have an apparitional existence than men? Female apparitions are undoubtedly more prolific than their male counterparts. I have often wondered why, but have never heard any particularly good explanation.

Many female phantoms seem to be linked to events of a tragic nature. It is a sobering thought that, in many instances, they are linked to cases of rape, suicide, and murder. Another characteristic of female apparitions is that they tend to manifest in colour and not in black and white, or even sepia tones. Often however, if the reports are to be believed, they often seem to manifest in a single colour. I have come across white ladies, grey ladies, green ladies, blue ladies, and even one pink lady. Grey, white, and semi-transparent ladies are legion, and one wonders, harking back to matters of energy, whether it may be more difficult to manifest in other colours. Is colour indicative of character, or some other trait? Do white ladies tend to be nice, and blue ladies tend to be slightly scary? A colleague of mine believes that the colour tones are likely to be more in the eye of the beholder than in the 'energy' seen. But if this is so, why do so many people who have seen a certain apparition seem to see it in the same colour? So many questions, so few answers...

Some thirty years ago, the Rev. D.S., a young Church of Ireland curate told me that he had seen a blue lady. He had seen her quite distinctly on a number of occasions at various times of the day. He was embarrassed at having to make this disclosure, as if it somehow it impugned his faith or clashed with his calling. I must confess that I found this a little testing. Why is it that so many clergymen are reluctant to preserve an open mind towards the paranormal? One would have thought that they, of all people, would have had a modicum of understanding?

The young man had just recently moved to Donaghadee. His house was in the process of being refurbished and in the meantime he had been lodging with the rector and his family. On his first evening, as he and the rector's family sat at dinner, a woman entered the room, clad in a flowing, bluish gown, and took up position in the bay alcove.

No one acknowledged her, and she made no attempt to join the family at the table. Instead, she remained standing with her hands clasped and her gaze fixed upon him. This was no ethereal figure. She appeared largely three-dimensional, however there was a kind of 'misty' quality about her, which the curate put down to subdued lighting and the fact that she stood in shadow. After a while he realised that she had gone, although for the life of him he couldn't say when she had done so.

After this first encounter he saw her a number of times at different places in the house, mostly towards evening and always when he was by himself. He described her as 'looking a bit old fashioned' and having 'a sweet face'.

The curate discussed her with no one. And the fact that the family appeared to see nothing made his sense of isolation all the greater. The opportunity to broach the subject arose one dinner time when the rector's daughter, a trainee nurse, happened to mention that the Rectory was haunted. 'Did he believe in ghosts?' she asked him.

This was his cue. Out it all came.

'I'm sorry,' he said. 'I don't know what's happening to me. I've never hallucinated before.'

The girl's reply astonished him further.

'Oh you've seen the Blue Lady?' she said. 'We've all seen her. She's quite harmless. She just likes to greet visitors.' They discussed her as they might discuss a mutual acquaintance, or a slightly eccentric member of the congregation. The apparition predated them all. Her father had found mention of her in a journal kept by a predecessor.

'We think she's a former rector's wife,' she added, 'and that she loved the place so much she couldn't leave.' The young lady left the curate with his thoughts.

That evening they discussed her again.

'She's very fond of your floor,' she said. 'We think your room was her sewing room.' With this consoling thought in mind, the curate climbed the stairs to bed, and after having dutifully said his prayers, leapt into bed, turned out the light and no doubt pulled the sheet right over his head!

I have had several 'lady' experiences. Many years ago, more years than I care to remember, I encountered a very gentle lady. She manifested in a Norfolk dawn as I lay in bed in a fourteenth century half-timbered house, that in later life had become a vicarage. It stood in the most beautiful garden, which was dewy and mist-shrouded at that early hour.

I awoke on the first day of my holiday with a sensation of serenity and lightness of heart. Outside, the birds were singing their hearts out. I lay cosily in bed and listened.

Then, as I turned my head, out of the corner of my eye I noticed a movement against the latticed window. I concentrated on the window, where I saw a woman leaning against the wide window ledge. She appeared to be dressed in one of those grey morning wrappers that were so fashionable in early Victorian times, and her long fair hair fell loosely down her back. I lay there hardly daring to breathe lest I scared her away.

I felt no sense of apprehension or fear. An overwhelming sense of peace enfolded me. As she realised she was being observed, she slowly turned to face me. Then, under my enchanted gaze, her beautiful face broke into a smile. For a long moment we looked at one another. Then almost imperceptibly, she grew more and more translucent, until she had merged entirely into the curtain behind her. I slowly sat up in bed, aware that I was once more alone, and that my gentle visitor had disappeared.

I had a second 'lady' experience in Enniskillen, County Fermanagh, in the 1970s. The previous evening I had spoken at the local Woman's Institute, and rather than send me back to Belfast, one of the Committee members had very kindly invited me to be her guest overnight. I gratefully accepted, and after one of the famous W.I. suppers, retired to bed full of good cheer!

Next morning, as I had some travelling ahead of me, I woke quite early and went down to the dining room for breakfast. As I sat at my meal an elderly lady passed me. She paused momentarily at what had to be a mirror on the far wall, and then disappeared into a walk-in pantry at the end of the room. When Mrs McR, my hostess, joined me a minute or two later, I happened to mention that her mother was at work in the pantry. Smiling, Mrs McR shook her head. Her mother was on holiday.

'My mistake,' I apologised. 'I just thought she looked a bit like you.'

Mrs McR's smile broadened, 'That's Aunt Ellie,' she explained, 'she always comes to inspect visitors.'

With some nonchalance, she explained that 'Aunt Ellie' was a friendly family apparition, who could also be encountered on the bedroom corridor and in the garden. She is believed to have been the housekeeper in the late nineteenth century, when the place had been the home of a rather crusty bachelor.

'Not everyone sees her as plain as you did,' she added.

I had seen her plain. And there was something about the whole thing that was nagging at me. I retraced her movements in my mind. Then it hit me. She had stopped to check her hair in the dining room mirror. Which was all well and good. Except that there was no mirror. The mirror had been removed years before.

'She doesn't bother us,' Mrs McR continued, 'so we don't mind her. But she's a curious old body, and if we have a visitor, she always pays them a visit. I expect she got a bit lonely, with no other women in the house,' she remarked as she refilled my cup.

I expect she did!

The most famous 'lady' phantom in Ulster is probably 'the Grey Lady of Lambeg', who has been sighted in every generation for the last four hundred years. She walks the stretch of road from the big house in the centre of the village, known locally as 'the Chains', to the parish church. From here she is said to make her way to the Nun's Garden, the old graveyard and supposed burial place of the community of nuns that once lived here.

Although she seems to have a regular beat to the churchyard gate from the village, I did have one report of her materialising in a cottage opposite the church, and appearing to have misgivings about certain of the titles on the owner's bookshelf.

She is not the only spectre known in the village. Apparitions have reportedly been seen in the Aberdelghy development, which is said to have been built on the site of the old hospice. Footsteps have been heard in people's gardens, and in the 1970s a male apparition was reportedly seen by a housewife and a child on separate occasions.

However it is 'the Lady' that excites most interest. Alas, she has no name or history. The last sighting reported to me occurred about five years ago. A taxi driver waiting to collect a passenger after the morning service saw a 'lady' standing silently outside the church porch. She appeared not to notice him. She was dressed, he said, in long grey garments and a black hood. After a short while she faded away, and a very sober taxi driver collected his fare and made what speed he could for the village. Thankfully, she did not appear to want a lift!

The Gypsy & the Baby

Ghosts or apparitions come in many shapes and forms. They may be of solid matter, opaque or only partially visible. They may be seen in broad daylight, and may follow a set pattern of behaviour, i.e. walk down a staircase. They may appear only on anniversaries, that is to say be capable of perception only on a certain date. Very few seem to have free movement. Most seem to be tied to or bound up with a particular place. Some apparitions appear unaware that they have an audience. They move like figures in a silent film, unable to be spoken to or contacted. Others seem capable of conscious thought. They intervene in the present, sometimes to pass on a warning. This may occur in the case of a death visitation, when the apparition seeks out someone specific (see Signs and Portents*). Occasionally the apparition 'needs a favour' and wants something done by the living that they cannot do themselves (see* Haddock's Ghost*).*

I have always treated information about apparitions with great caution, no matter where it comes from. Stories can improve with the telling. They can acquire shape and detail that was not originally there. But relatively few people who have seen apparitions consciously embroider. They want explanations. Answers. And they are usually careful to pass on the experience as it occurred to them in order to get them.

In the year 1976 I received two reports from motorists using the Upper Malone Road near to the gates of Lady Dixon Park in Belfast. The reports differed very little in content and one could see how they would be extremely upsetting. The gist of the information was that, in the early evening, when passing along this road, the driver would see what he took to be a 'travelling woman' standing at the roadside, nursing an infant wrapped in a shawl. As the motorist approached she would suddenly rush into the road and appear to hurl herself at the car. Sometimes the horrified motorist would see the woman and a bundle of rags actually pass over the bonnet, and fall to the ground on the passenger side of the car.

Shocked beyond belief at what appeared to be a suicide attempt, the motorist would brake hard, get out and run round to the other side of the car, dreading what he would find. To his astonishment there would be absolutely nothing there; the woman and baby had vanished. There was a particularly harrowing account given to me on the telephone one night by a distraught young man, who had been involved in such an incident. His fiancé was in the car with him and she also appeared to have witnessed the whole thing.

'She's hysterical,' the young man told me. 'I can't do a thing with her, and there's no one else about. I'm phoning from a box along the road a bit.'

I tried to calm him down, wondering meantime how he had got my number, as I wasn't aware of knowing him. Later it turned out that he and his girlfriend had attended talks that I had given at the College of Further Education in Belfast, and that he still had a flyer advertising the course in the car. Anyway, I told him that I would contact the police, and explain the circumstances as best I could.

'Is she OK? Does she have a medical condition?' I enquired anxiously, having visions of the need for an ambulance.

'If she hasn't one now, she certainly will have,' came the grim reply. 'She's petrified and so am I.'

I contacted the police, and was amazed to learn that the local constabulary had already heard about 'the gipsy and the baby' from another motorist. They assured me that they would dispatch a car at once, as they already knew my line of work from one or two encounters we had shared before.

When the tally of horrified motorists had reached five, I felt it was time to do a little detective work myself. The road was an ancient routeway. Much of it had been realigned over the years,

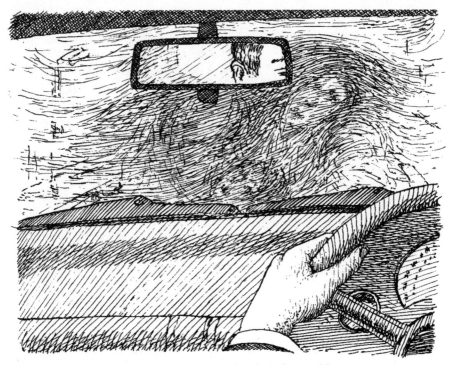

'As the motorist approached she would
suddenly... hurl herself at the car'

but not this part, which was 'original' and would have carried
the traffic of centuries.

Who was the mysterious, ragged 'gypsy woman'? Had she died
here? Had her child perhaps died here, by the roadside, in want
and destitution, ignored by passers by? Had the father of her
child died here? Was he perhaps one of the miserable 'footpads'
who preyed on the travellers that used the road, a petty criminal
who had been caught and executed here at the scene of his crime?
The gypsy woman's reckless behaviour was also surely significant.
I felt that I was probably dealing with a suicide. But why? The
question tormented me. What wrong or injustice had driven her
to hurl herself and her young child under the wheels of a passing
vehicle?

The horrid enactment of such a tragedy would for a time have
'infected' (for want of a better word) the whole area with the

crazed and despairing persona of the wretched woman. What had activated the 'replay' after a possible lapse of centuries I couldn't guess. But often some new disturbance can trigger the psychic recollection of an earlier tragedy. Then once more the waters of forgetfulness close over and the memory is lost.

This apparition was active for a number of months then disappeared, and to my knowledge has not again been sighted.

There was a curious sequel.

One late summer afternoon about six months after the incidents had ceased, my husband and I were coming home along this stretch of road. In the autumn the road at this point would be prone to mists, but this afternoon we could see clearly for hundreds of yards down towards the parish church of Drumbeg.

All of a sudden a patch of mist began to form in the road in front of us. As it thickened it seemed to take the form of a long sinuous body, which appeared to float towards our windscreen. I thought I could even detect the moulding of an indistinct face. My husband braked sharply and the 'mist' rapidly rolled over the top of the car, making, as it were, for the road behind us.

I got out of the car but the road was quite clear. There was no sign of the 'mist' anywhere, and we were the only ones on the road. I looked at Stanley and he nodded.

'I know what you're going to say,' he muttered. 'Well, just don't say it!'

Getting back into the car, I had the wisdom to keep my thoughts to myself.

The Abbey Scholar

One particular fallacy beloved of ghost story writers is that the best time to view ghostly happenings is at twilight, or in the gloom of graveyards. Most apparitions, they will tell you, are wraith-like creatures who utter weird shrieks or carry their heads under their arms. To that I say, not so!

Firstly, apparitions tend not to be encountered where people's bodies are buried, but where those people lived. Secondly, apparitions are often very substantial and 'life-like'. Most appear in broad daylight and do very normal things. And you can find them anywhere: in caravans, public toilets, and the back seats of cars! I also recall an instance of the haunting of a bingo hall, which undoubtedly makes for interesting conjecture.

The cases cited below are of this nature. The apparitions involved are dressed rather quaintly, but are quite normal in their looks and behaviour. As you will appreciate, this being so, more of us than we realise may have 'seen a ghost' at some time and not realised it until (or unless) the disincarnate visitor does something abnormal like walking through a closed door.

By and large, the older a site is, the more likely it is to have acquired some kind of psychic tier to its being. Religious sites tend to be particularly good at doing this. I like to think too that the sense of serenity that one can feel in religious places is also conducive to making psychic connections.

Greyabbey, in County Down, is one of my favourite religious sites. Here on the eastern bank of Strangford Lough, one can find the impressive and partially restored remains of the

Cistercian abbey founded in 1193 by Affreca, the wife of John de Courcy. The Abbey was dissolved in or around 1541-43.

That however, was not the end of it as a place of worship. In the early seventeenth century it was re-roofed, and it remained in use as the parish church until about 1778. Though age and various forms of vandalism have taken their toll, there is a lot still to see; and no one who knows these fine and extremely atmospheric gothic ruins will be completely surprised to learn that there have been reports of apparitions at the site.

I know of two reports of sightings, made by different people on separate summer evenings. The first came from a clergyman friend who was looking for a spot to take a photograph for the cover of his church magazine. He was sizing up the great West Door, when has saw a young man heading towards it along a well-trodden path. The youth was carrying a bundle of books secured by a strap holder.

'He looked quite preoccupied,' my friend reported, 'and seemed to be in a bit of a hurry. I can't say that I took particular note of his dress, save that it was black or grey in colour, and that his coat seemed overly long. To my astonishment, as he went into the church he seemed to grow fainter, until he vanished altogether. He had the look of a scholar and his hair was light and curly.'

My friend hurried in after him but found no sign of anyone. The place was empty. The young man had disappeared. My friend was mystified but felt no fear of what he now had to conclude was an apparition.

'I felt that he had some connection with the Abbey,' he suggested. 'Perhaps he was one of the novices?' And that camera. Had he taken a photograph? Of course he hadn't. I could have biffed him!

The second account of an apparition manifesting here came from a lecturer from Queens University, Belfast, who had been visiting in connection with work she was doing on medieval monastic foundations. She was just on her way out of the ruins, when in front of her she saw three ladies heading for the Abbey. They were dressed in light coloured summer gowns reminiscent of crinolines, and two of the ladies wore bonnets.

They passed within yards of the departing Queenswoman, chattering and laughing together, and sharing great good feeling. Their dress was a little odd but she noticed nothing seriously unusual about them until she realised that, although they were chatting in the most animated fashion, they seemed to be making no sound. This realisation produced no fear. No consternation. Just intense interest.

Like the 'scholar', the ladies seemed completely absorbed in what they were doing. Unlike the 'scholar', these visitors did not dematerialise, but, looking very solid and three dimensional, disappeared quite normally into the Abbey. How then, you may say, did the woman who saw them know that they were apparitions? I asked her the same question, and the answer was swiftly forthcoming.

'Because their legs and feet disappeared just above the ankles, and the hems of their gowns were sort of misty and ethereal.'

They had no feet. They sort of glided along – a fairly common observation when the movement of apparitions is being described. Finally, I asked my witness about her feelings on witnessing the event. She considered the question for a moment then said very thoughtfully,

'I had the feeling that it was me who was the intruder, and that these women were going about their lawful business.' As indeed perhaps they were. Greyabbey was a favourite haunt of day-trippers in the eighteenth and nineteenth century, and these ladies were obviously enjoying every minute of their visit.

I too am drawn to abbeys and old church sites. One lovely summer's afternoon in 1989, a companion and I were walking beside the quiet waters of the River Quoile at Inch Abbey, near Downpatrick. We were taking pictures and notes for a newspaper article on the Abbey. What bliss it is to be paid for doing something one loves doing!

While my companion was photographing the Abbey ruins, I went down to the river. As I enjoyed the loveliness of the scene, I noticed a small boat containing three men come round a bend in the river and head past me. I took the men to be anglers. They wore rough jerseys, and seemed very involved with the management of their craft. They seemed to be looking for a spot on the nearby headland on which to land.

After a moment or so, the boat drifted round the headland and out of sight. As I could see the far side of the headland, I fully expected that in a minute or so, the boat would re-emerge and continue its leisurely progress along the river; or that, when they had tied up the boat, out of my sight, I would see the men come ashore. I waited and waited, and was baffled by the fact that neither of these things happened.

As I puzzled over this, I saw two men strolling towards me along the river bank. It seemed inconceivable that they would not have seen the men in the boat. As they bade me good afternoon, I decided to ask them if the little boat had made a safe landing. They looked at me in a puzzled fashion.

'What boat?' they chorused.

'A little rowing boat. With three men in it.' The men looked confused. The older man grinned.

'Perhaps you saw the brothers out fishing?' he drawled. 'Aye. Maybe you saw the brothers.'

His companion nodded.

'They do say some folks see them.'

'You didn't see a boat?' I persisted. I had to be clear about this. Even at the risk of trying their patience. Both shook their heads.

'I'm sorry,' said the first man, 'I wish I had!' Then they strolled on past me in the direction from which I had come.

As I struggled to make sense of this mysterious reply, my companion rejoined me, his photographs taken. He received a similar interrogation. He also replied in the negative. He had been in the ruins, not watching the river. And there the matter lay.

About five months later, I was giving a lecture in Belfast when I happened on a colleague who lived in the Downpatrick area. I told her my story.

'That's very odd,' she said. 'The same thing happened to me.

In the exact same spot. I saw three men in a rowing boat. I thought they were fishing, and they disappeared round the headland too.' I asked her if there'd been any other witnesses.

'You know, its funny you should ask,' she said. 'My husband was with me. I asked him if he thought the men were fishing? "What men?" he replied.

And so we were both back to square one. We both knew that we'd seen the same thing on the river, and we both agreed that the best explanation was that we had probably seen 'the brothers' going about their daily work. My friend added that the third man, in the stern of the vessel, seemed much younger than the other two. We had of course no idea how many people had seen them and remained silent, but it is an interesting thought! Another interesting point is that, in both instances, 'not seeing' had been as important as 'seeing' in revealing the true character of the event. Had everyone seen the little boat, no one would probably have thought any more about it.

But what had we seen? Was it another 'time slip'? Had we seen the brothers in their own time, performing a real task? Or had something emerged from our subconscious minds, coaxed out by our sensitivity to the ethos of the site? And if so, why the same thing? Sightings at places like abbeys are quite frequent. However, for two people, at different times, to have seen the same thing is not.

A Moment in Time

Paranormal manifestations can be fleeting. 'Blink your eye', and you may miss them. People who have seen apparitions have regularly told me that they, 'didn't have time to be scared, it happened so quickly.' Sadly, many people who have had a paranormal experience don't realise it until afterwards, by which time many salient details may have been forgotten. Some though, get enough time, or are lucky enough to take it all in ...

Every morning Robert McC made the journey from his home in Banbridge to his work in Newry, where he was assistant manager in the local branch of the Bank of Ireland. He liked to travel early to avoid the traffic. Just before 8.00 am one May morning in 1970, Robert was driving to work as usual. The road lay open before him, and he was in a relaxed and contented frame of mind.

As he rounded a bend, he saw the figure of a man on the verge on the passenger side, about a hundred metres distant. The figure did not appear to be soliciting a lift. It was as though he was waiting for someone.

As Robert came closer, he could see that the man was wearing a military uniform, but carrying no weapon. This was unusual, when you consider the times. In 1970 uniformed soldiers were only seen on guard or on patrol duty, and then in groups of three or four at a minimum. This man was alone, and all he carried was a kit bag slung over his shoulder, and what appeared to be a gas mask case.

Robert had served as a sergeant with the Royal Engineers in

World War Two, and was familiar with military uniforms. As he got closer, he noticed that, in spite of the mildness of the morning, the figure was wearing a heavy army greatcoat and a forage cap, and that his feet were encased in heavy army boots, and puttees or leggings.

'I probably wouldn't have been so observant,' he said, as he told me the story, 'but I had slowed down in case he needed a lift. I thought he'd missed the bus or something.' However, far from appearing to see the approaching car, the man ignored Robert; but his face was not expressionless, he seemed to be looking for someone.

The car drove some fifty metres beyond the figure, which Robert recalled later seemed perfectly three dimensional and of natural colour. In fact the man's face was very youthful and fresh looking. He seemed to be in the best of health. All at once, Robert looked in his driving mirror, and saw to his astonishment that the verge behind him was now empty. The soldier had disappeared.

Robert braked sharply and got out of the car. He walked back, but there was no one to be seen. There were no gateways or lanes, and the nearest house was about a quarter of a mile away, beyond where he had parked his car.

Baffled and a little alarmed, Robert scanned both sides of the road. There was no one there. The figure had gone. It was a sober and worried man who drove the rest of the way to Newry, debating whether or not to report his sighting, and if he did, what he should say. In the end he told only his wife, and a few years later, me.

'What was the point in reporting it?' he protested, 'who would have believed me?

As he drove on, a door in his mind slowly opened. The man had been dressed in soldier's uniform, but not the mottled fatigues we are used to. This soldier was wearing older army dress, and he was carrying a gas mask and a kitbag. It was then, with a shiver, that Robert was hit with the certainty that he had seen a vision from the past. Maybe the soldier was a local lad. Maybe he got a lift to Newry, when he was returning from or coming on leave? Maybe he was standing at the roadside looking for his regular lift? The experience left him with nothing but questions.

Another person who had time to evaluate what she saw was Mrs D from Belfast, who in October 1958 saw an apparition in Alexandra Park, Belfast.

'I was on my way back from the shops one afternoon, walking down Castleton Gardens beside the park,' she said, 'when I noticed a woman coming out of Jubilee Avenue, from the Antrim Road. As I watched she crossed the road, went into the park, walked down the path and vanished. And that was a bit of a shock I can tell you!' I agreed that it must have been.

'When I got to the gates she had passed through, they were locked,' she continued. 'That was my second shock. It was five o'clock by my watch. It must have been closing time. Even before she disappeared she had caught my eye because she was wearing a black shawl over her shoulders and a long white skirt. Later, after I'd seen old photographs of linen workers, I discovered that this was probably not a skirt, but a type of wrap-around apron worn by the spinners in the mills before the First World War. There would have been quite a few mills round here once.'

Her sighting, I felt, had all the hallmarks of a 'film clip' apparition (see *The Abbey Scholar*), which some theorists would explain as a negative print in the 'ether' which becomes positive in the presence of someone with ESP, who at that moment happens to be receptive, and then 'replays' like a clip from a movie film. I am agnostic about this and most of the other theories which have been advanced to explain apparitions. Most, quite frankly, are inadequate. But I am not particularly troubled by their inadequacy. The fact that at the moment we don't have all the answers is not relevant. In time they will come. One day perhaps we will know as much about the mechanics of the paranormal as we do about electricity or atomic power.

A third such apparition was seen near Hilltown in south Down in 1974 by Mr S.T. when he was out walking his greyhound in the fields behind his farm.

Shortly after the pair had left the house, the rest of the family heard scratching at the door, and the frightened whine of the greyhound, asking to be let in. They were surprised. The dog enjoyed its walks, and it had been out for no more than a few minutes.

The walk had taken them up the fields towards the old family homestead, now in ruins. To reach it they crossed two fields, which were linked by a gap in the hedge. As the man approached the gap, with the dog running here and there ahead of him, a small, elderly woman in black, with a printed apron across her dress, came into view. The presence of the woman was unusual in itself, for no one but the family was ever round there. She seemed 'busy', so he didn't try to greet her. As the gap was small, and the woman would reach it first, he slowed down to let her through.

But some yards from the gap she disappeared, and the dog let out an unnatural yelp and took off across the field as if all the demons in hell were after him. The owner returned to the house to find the dog lying shivering under the table. For days it refused all food and would not leave the house. The normally courageous and placid animal was terrified out of its wits.

It so happened that I had some involvement at that time with the sport of greyhound racing, and by chance was introduced to the owner of the frightened dog, which was called King's Reach, and was a very promising racer. I knew the dog well, indeed I had won money on it, and felt it had a great future. Mr S.T. told me the story. Who, I wondered, did he think he might have seen? His belief was that the old woman was someone who lived in the vicinity of the farm in his grandfather's time. The idea that he might have come face to face with one of his forebearers, was I think, a little too hot to handle! And what of his poor dog?

'That dog was a great animal,' he told me, 'but after he saw the old woman, he never did any good, he was that nervous. And he never went through the gap again. You had to lift and carry him.' The fact that animals are sensitive to the paranormal is well known, but is seldom so clearly demonstrated.

The Narrow Water Castle Massacre

The Narrow Water Castle story is a classic 'time slip' experience. It is a sobering story, made all the grimmer by the way it links the paranormal with the savage politics of this place. It has pathos too, because of the way in which the Narrow Water manifestations appear to give lives tragically cut short in the Troubles a kind of melancholy, mechanical continuity.

What follows is the account as it was given to me. It is as accurate as I can make it.

One evening in 1980, Mr T.M., a middle-aged businessman, was driving home to Rostrevor along the road beside Carlingford Lough. It was a journey made each day from Warrenpoint, and the road was very familiar to him. He had never had a paranormal experience before, nor I believe has he had one since, and for him travelling home that night beside the lough was an everyday experience, one that with hindsight he would never forget.

The road took him past Narrow Water Castle, a medieval tower house that had originally belonged to the Magennis chiefs. This bold, confident building stands on the loughside, commanding fine views towards the sea. The castle was at one time said to be haunted by the apparition of a girl, who had thrown herself from the top of the tower into the lough after her young lover drowned in its icy waters. There are several accounts of this earlier tragedy, but it has no connection with the dreadful massacre that took place near the castle walls in the course of our most recent troubles.

In August 1979, a unit of soldiers on checkpoint duty near the castle were ambushed and blown up by the IRA. That awful night, eighteen young men were brutally murdered in what came to be known as 'the Narrow Water Castle massacre'.

Over a year later, but not on the anniversary of the atrocity, Mr T.M. was driving by as usual, steeped in his thoughts, when:

'Suddenly on the road ahead of me I saw an arc of light, like the one that would come from a powerful torch being swung round and round by hand.'

I was listening together with some of his neighbours. We all knew what he meant, as the torch was used by the security forces to let cars know that there was a check point ahead. This required one to dip one's headlights and slowly come to a stop and show one's driving licence or some other means of identification. I had indeed come through just such a check that very evening on my way to see Mr T.M.

Mr T.M. complied with the procedure. A soldier came to his car window. He saw other figures moving about under the trees. He thought he saw weapons. He assumed that his driving licence was in demand, at least he had the sensation of someone asking for it, and so he rummaged about for it and handed it out the window, before complying with a second request to open the boot. Now unsure as to whether he had actually heard a voice or heard 'something in his head', Mr T.M. got out.

Followed by the soldier, he went round and opened the boot. Almost immediately, he began to feel cold and uncomfortable. When he stood back, his companion was nowhere to be seen. Somewhat nonplussed, he went back to the driver's door, only to find his driving licence on the ground, and the road around him empty and windswept. Where was the soldier? Where were the other soldiers he was sure he had seen moving about under the trees? There was no one there except himself.

A chill and numbing sense of horror took hold of him. He bundled himself into the still warm car and drove off. It should be added that he was entirely sober and in full possession of his faculties when this incident took place. Try as he would, he could find no rational explanation for what had happened to him, but

'Suddenly on the road ahead of me I saw an arc of light...'

he knew what he has seen, and recalled the incident of the massacre a year earlier.

Between June 1980 and March 1981 two other similar incidents were reported. On each occasion there was more than one person in the car. These witnesses vouched that they had seen the solitary soldier, that the car boot had been opened and that the figure had then vanished, just as in T.M.'s case. They could also corroborate T.M.'s impression of 'men moving about under the trees'.

The massacre had been a traumatic event for the local community, and as one they came together to hold a vigil at the spot, at which prayers and rosaries were said. This action must have been 'cleansing'. But evidently it was not cleansing enough. After about three years, however, there were no more reports of phantom soldiers at the site, and there have been none now for over fourteen years. I know also of several psychic 'sensitives' who drove the route in the hope of making contact with these 'phantoms', but their journeys were without incident. One can only hope that those tragic souls now rest in peace.

Whatever initiated this macabre happening is a matter for conjecture. We have no means of identifying the lone soldier, nor would I wish to. All I can say is that a number of motorists, whose minds seem to have been relaxed and in a state of rest, picked up forceful vibrations from a spot on the road that had been the site of a traumatic experience. Vibrations strong enough to have form, and to have intervened in contemporary 'reality'.

'I would never ever want to experience anything like that again. I can still feel the chill that ran through me, and that feeling of being completely alone,' Mr T.M. told me, grateful to have left 'the paranormal' behind him, and to have brushed up against it only once.

The Power of Touch

For centuries we have had great faith in the power of touch. Monarchs used to be credited with the power to cure diseases like leprosy by merely extending their hands to the sufferer. Faith healers set great store by touch, as do some Christian denominations, whose ministers obey the divine injunction to heal the sick through 'the laying on of hands', after the example of the wonderful miracles of Jesus of Nazareth.

When spiritualists link hands, the power of touch is believed to increase the energy within the circle and increase the possibility of communicating with the spirits of the departed, if such there are.

My favourite local instance of the mysterious power of touch is an account given to me in the 1960s by W.J.D., a quiet spoken, middle-aged farmer from near Ballygawley in south Tyrone, of a brief but memorable experience that he had when he was a boy.

'I had been walking home with my sister Lizzie,' he explained, 'and on the way we passed the remains of a chapel, now in ruins. As we passed it I became aware of a figure in the doorway. He was tall and wore a friar's robe that reached to his ankles. His head was covered by a hood.' He smiled, 'I don't mind telling you I was scared. But the man had a kind face and was smiling, and he made no attempt to come closer. "See the man?" I asked my sister in a low voice, not sure, I suppose, whether to treat him as a person or a 'thing'. "What man?" she said, staring straight through him.'

'I couldn't understand, so I pointed, "Him there," I said. She kept looking but it was clear she saw no one. In exasperation I took her hand and said in my loudest whisper, "That man, in the doorway." Her face paled and she clung to me. "I do." And she set off up the lane as fast as her legs would carry her. Then I took fright and did the same!'

He smiled at me a little shame-facedly. 'I'm not normally a feardie,' he said, 'but when I realised that until I touched her, she couldn't see the man, my hair fairly stood on end.' I explained that I thought that, in touching his sister, he had communicated his vision to her, enabling her to see what he could see. He looked quite relieved. 'I thought I might be doing something bad,' he confessed. 'You see, I'd never seen a ghost before.' He paused. 'It was one, wasn't it?'

That was quite a question. Just what had he seen? I felt the likeliest explanation was that it was a 'silent film' apparition; a stray piece of footage of someone who had known or worshipped in the place. It might not even have been aware of him. But then again, it might not have been a 'replay'. It might have been alive at another time, and gone on to resume its life, just as he and his sister had gone on to resume theirs. This was an enigmatic and instructive experience, but not a sinister one, and I thought that W.J.D. had coped with it well. Perhaps surprisingly, given his extra sensory capabilities, he has had no paranormal experiences since.

The Lost Boy

Nothing better illustrates the power of touch than psychometry, the technique of finding out things about people by touching or handling items belonging to them. It works best when the object used is special to the person, for instance a favourite watch or a wedding ring.

The technique can produce results, though no one is very clear why. Some believe that the object used acts as a focal point for the exercise of extra sensory perception. Others think that it carries a 'psychic residue' which can give veridical information about its owner. Another similar idea is that frequently worn objects absorb the bodily aura and give off the same 'vibrations'.

Psychometry is also used in entertainment. The magician asks members of the audience to send up items like watches and rings. In a matter of moments he will connect the object to its owner, revealing very personal information about them, to the owner's embarrassment and the audience's delight.

I have only tried to identify an object once, when a friend asked me to close my eyes and tell him where it came from. I did so, without much hope of being right. To my surprise, when I held the object in my hand I felt ninety-five per cent sure where it had originated.

'It's from Gill Hall in Dromore,' I said. 'It's a piece of glass, possibly from the front door.' To my amusement, my enquirer and his friend exchanged cash.

'I knew she would know,' said one of them in triumph. I am glad to say that I have never been tested in this way since. I felt no weird sensation. I went neither hot nor cold, or dizzy. All I felt was an unmistakable sensation of knowing, and no hesitation in speaking up.

Shortly afterwards, I was to see the same technique applied in police work, in a very unhappy case which was to end in tragedy. If one wanted to develop this kind of psychic gift one would need to be strong enough to take the rough with the smooth.

A police inspector of my acquaintance had invited me to sit in on a psychometrist's deliberations, and I readily agreed. A young boy had gone missing. Several weeks had passed and there had been no clues as to his whereabouts. The fields about his home were searched, the river was dragged, but nothing had come to light.

The anguished parents consulted their minister, who suggested that they perhaps seek the help of a clairvoyant or medium. The father was not happy with this idea, but the missing boy's mother was so desperate she would have tried anything. Northern Ireland is not overly blessed with top quality mediums, so the family were put in contact with a Scottish medium, who agreed to help.

She asked for a piece of clothing or a favourite toy to work with. The boy's mother gave her a tee shirt, and the teddy bear that he had had almost since birth. Sitting in his home, closing her eyes, the medium handled the two objects. Then she frowned. She began speaking in disjointed sentences:

'I see a stretch of road... there's a river over a hedge... and a weir... lots of tree stumps in the water, or logs... floating... one is caught in the weir... and I see a bundle of rags... drifting up and down with the water.' She added that she didn't feel that anyone else had been involved. That seemed to be all she could 'see'. And it didn't really lift our mood because we all knew that the river, four or five hundred metres away at the back of the estate, had already been thoroughly searched by police divers.

The mother begged the inspector to search the river again. He was reluctant. That avenue had been explored and yielded nothing. But he agreed. Just in case. So the next day police divers searched the river near the weir, which carried an enormous flow of water. One of the divers saw what he took to be 'a bundle of rags' attached to a rotting log... the little boy had been found.

No one will ever know how he got into the river, which was quite well fenced, but the post mortem revealed that he must have been in there almost since his disappearance. At last his mother and father had a body to grieve over, and they were able to draw some peace of mind from the fact that their son had died as a result of a tragic accident, with no one else involved.

I remember thinking how tired and drained the medium looked afterwards. What she had done had cost her dearly, and I remember feeling truly relieved that I had not been endowed with her gifts.

Matters Left Undone

This account transcends the paranormal, leaving us in another dimension entirely. Some of its elements are familiar – a house that seems to exist in perpetual shadow, a place that depressed and undermined the well-being of the person who lived there. Places are sometimes described as 'unwelcoming'. The house that we are about to visit was more than unwelcoming. It resented and rejected its owner. The change that came over it was miraculous.

A telephone call one May afternoon alerted me to the fact that someone was in trouble, and that the house he lived in was the problem. I agreed to go and see him. Mr A.N. had recently arrived here from the Home Counties in order to take up a new job. He was unmarried, and had bought the house sight unseen on the recommendation of a well-known estate agent. At first he was delighted. The house was everything he had hoped for, and he lost no time in settling in.

His new home was a neat, detached, modern dwelling (a handy reminder that not all 'haunted' houses are ancient, cob-webbed piles!) It had a pleasant, sunny situation in a prosperous part of Dunmurry, just outside Belfast. The previous occupants had been a young couple who had maintained the property well.

For the first few weeks everything seemed very normal. He got busy in the garden. He thought about doing some redecorating. Slowly, however, it dawned on him that all might not be well.

'I gradually realised that when I came home from work of an

evening that I didn't feel quite alone. I just sensed something about the place. It was as though it was under an invisible cloud. I'm not fanciful. I'm not religious. I'm used to working under stress, and not letting things get to me,' he said, 'yet slowly and insidiously the house began to depress me.'

'I started making excuses for not going straight home after work. I'd stop off to have a meal in a pub, or call in on a friend. And that's not me. I like cooking for myself.' He smiled, 'yet the minute the key went into the lock I felt that someone had got there before me. I felt unwanted in my own home.'

'I had called to see A.N. with a colleague. As I glanced around the room I saw he'd completed his decoration. The room was freshly papered and painted. It looked great, and we picked up no hint of the 'cloud' he talked of. It is true that the house was a little on the chilly side, but it was empty most of the day, so that was hardly to be wondered at. I asked if he felt uncomfortable all over the house or just in specific places?

'This room's the worst,' he said. Here by my chair, and over by the door. Sometimes it's as though something's looking over my shoulder. It's not just me either. I have a friend who brings his boxer dog over with him, and its forever trying to get out. It crawls round this room on its belly and keeps whining. I think it might be seeing something.'

A.N. told of others who had come to stay and felt similar kinds of discomfort. 'Its also on the stairs, outside the bathroom door, and in one of the front bedrooms – but nowhere as bad as here.' I noticed my colleague involuntarily button up his coat and move a little closer to the heater. A.N. apologised for bringing us out. I assured him that we were more than glad to try to help.

I was impressed with A.N. He struck me as a very reasonable and intelligent man. He had also made one or two careful enquiries of his neighbours, but had been told of nothing unusual. He had, he admitted, considered moving, but was blowed if he was going to be turned out of his own house!

Both my colleague and myself had come across this worrying syndrome before. We both knew of a man who might be able to help. He was a minister in the Church of Ireland who had conducted several successful 'exorcisms'. Not that he saw them as that. He saw them as healings by prayer and communion. When called, he had come to the troubled house, offered prayers in every room, and held a simple communion service in the main living room. I don't normally like mixing religion with the paranormal, but there are times when it seems right to do so. And this was one.

A.N. had no objection to me speaking to our friend. Matters were arranged the following week and I left for a lecture tour. Before I left I learned a very significant fact. The couple who lived in the house before had had the wife's mother living with them. Relations in the house had been stormy. One morning after a particularly bitter row, the mother had rushed onto the road, and been knocked down and killed.

I told this to my priestly friend, who paused reflectively,

'This could be the root of this trouble,' he said. 'Some words or an action left undone.'

This made me think, how true. When someone is suddenly taken from us before we have time to call back a hasty word or an unkind action, we can indeed suffer agonies of remorse. Here were three people who had no time to make up their quarrel before tragedy intervened.

A week later when I got back from my trip, I had a message from A.N. asking me to phone him. The man who answered the phone was a different being from the one I had left. He was overflowing with excitement.

'It worked,' he said. 'Your clergyman friend did a great job.'

The minister, with an aide and my colleague, had visited the house, and celebrated Holy Communion. He had spoken on the need to forgive, and be at peace with one another. It seemed that he had more of a feeling than we can know that the grief and regret of all the parties had poisoned the atmosphere. Somehow, the grief seemed to have been purged.

'It's like a new house,' enthused A.N. 'It's as though the house can breathe again. I felt the difference almost immediately. The place felt warmer and friendlier. And now when I get in I really feel I'm coming home. I shan't move now,' he said. 'That stuff's over. Everything's OK.'

He invited me round. I sensed the change right away. Everything was cosy again. And it was nice for once to have a happy ending.

The Sandiman Port Man

*Invermore House, near Larne in County Antrim, was built by the
Casement family in the early nineteenth century. Its most celebrated visitor
is believed to have been Roger Casement, later executed for his involvement
in the 1916 rising. He is said to have holidayed here, and we shall hear
more of him shortly. The house was then occupied by Howdens and Fishers,
and passed out of single ownership in 1982, after which it was converted
into flats. I was privileged to know the last owner, a Miss McClane, and
her two charming companions, the Miss Thompsons, along with their
very lively canine menagerie.*

Invermore House first came to my notice in 1981, when one of
the Miss Thompsons phoned me to discuss certain curious
'happenings' that had taken place there. On the afternoon she
rang me, one occurred even while we spoke. The conversation
was going quite normally when, all of a sudden, I heard a heavy
door slam, and assumed that someone had just come into the
house. Miss Thompson excused herself and went to greet the
new arrival. When she returned to the phone she sounded
perplexed and upset.

'Did you hear a door slam?' she asked me. I said that I had.

'There was no-one there,' she added baldly.

'It's always happening. You think someone's come in. You go
to meet them and you find that you're the only one in the house.'
She sounded weary. I suggested that if it suited her, I could pay
them a visit next week, and that she and her companions could
tell me the whole story.

So the next week found me in Larne, driving up the long gravelled drive to the gracious old house. I was in possession of the basic facts. I had familiarised myself with the house's history. I was aware that during the 1840s a pair of funereal urns had been dug up in the garden, but I could make no link between these and the present disturbances. These were apparitional, clairaudient and poltergeistic. They occurred on a regular basis and all the residents of the house were aware of them, singly and together. The same may also have been true of their canine 'family', but one can only guess at this! The ladies were in early and late middle age, and appeared to be both practical and unflappable.

'We have seen the late owner of the house in the drawing room,' said Miss McClane, almost matter of factly. 'I have seen her twice, for a brief moment.' All three ladies had also experienced doors that slammed when locked, and they were the only people in the house. A handyman cum family acquaintance who did regular work for them had heard female voices upstairs in the house when he knew it to be empty. Assuming that his employers had come back unexpectedly, he had called up to them; whereupon a silence settled on the house, and he went on to discover that there was no one there but himself. He had also experienced an intense cold in the bedroom he occasionally used when staying over in the course of his work. He flatly refused to change rooms, even though it was patently clear that the experience of sleeping there made him uneasy.

The others were just the same. No one in the house was going to be put out by these provocations. At least they were determined not to be. However staying unruffled was clearly becoming a strain. And no wonder! In addition to the difficulties mentioned above, cupboards in various rooms had been ransacked, items of furniture had been shifted, and the usual variety of footsteps, of people and animals, had been heard in various corridors, particularly on the bedroom floor. Then matters had got worse.

As well as the apparition of the dead former owner, Miss McClane had seen an extremely striking apparition on the landing outside her bedroom door on more than one occasion.

'I see him,' she said, 'between my room and the bathroom door at night. He stands quite still by the wall, but I have to pass him, both coming and going from my room.'

I asked her what the apparition looked like.

'He reminds me of "the Sandiman Port man" in the advert,' she said unexpectedly.

'He wears an evening cloak and a broad brimmed hat. Oh, and he has a small beard.'

Miss McClane expressed the opinion that his dress was that of a gentleman in nineteenth century evening wear, and that he bore a striking resemblance to Sir Roger Casement. She further expressed the idea that in some curious way he was aware of her, and that a form of communication – which she could not put into words – took place between them. Unfortunately, from my point of view, none of the others had seen this 'gentleman', who appeared for a duration of at least several minutes, and almost always at night.

I marvelled at this sturdy woman's courage. Discovering and walking past 'Sir Roger' was one thing. But walking back, in the full knowledge that 'he' would be there waiting for her, was something else again. No question about it, the lady had guts! Why Sir Roger Casement should haunt a house which he had relatively little association with is a mystery to me, unless it could have had something to do with his being particularly happy and untroubled here.

Then came the night when all three ladies experienced the call of a bansidhe. The first time they heard the weird noise, it seemed to come from a hedge at the bottom of the garden, and went on for some time. Bansidhe are commonly heard out of doors so there was nothing unusual in the locale. The second time, however, one of the group heard it in the bedroom.

'I felt my flesh creep,' she confessed. 'Although I had never heard, and much less believed in that sort of thing before, I knew instinctively what it was,' she said. I assured her that this was a common occurrence.

The noise, which ranged from a low 'keening' to an eldritch shriek, lasted about forty minutes, during which time none of the women were inclined to get out of bed, although they had by then all retreated into the one room for company. The dogs slept through everything. I mentioned that there were two unusual aspects to this bansidhe's calling. One was that it was unusual to hear it in the house, and the second was that, in as far as the ladies knew, its calling was not connected to a death. Although there was an aunt in hospital, she recovered from her illness. One of the Miss Thompsons said that they had found the crying 'pitiful', and had felt very sorry for the creature. A rather charitable notion, I thought. After this nothing exceptional happened for some time, and after a while the house seemed once more to be at peace.

Their distress call to me came in the middle of a subsequent flare up of activity. I visited the house three times in all, and was, I think, able to reassure the ladies that they were not in any danger or mentally unstable, another common fear. At least I hope I did. They moved shortly afterwards, but I did not keep in touch, so I do not know exactly why.

There was a curious addendum to our discussion. On arriving I had left the car on the gravel drive at the front of the house, pointing towards the gate. The brake was on and the car was locked. Upon returning to the car, I was baffled to find that the driverless vehicle had executed a sharp right turn onto the grass verge, and had come to rest a few yards from a large greenhouse! The car was still locked and the brake still on. How it had mounted a fairly elevated verge all by itself, in full view of the house in broad daylight is a matter for considerable thought! In the somewhat mortified silence that followed, I retrieved my car and set out on my way.

A House Possessed

'Possessed' houses are mercifully few and far between. In my experience haunted people are rather more common than haunted places. However haunted is not really the right word. 'Psychically receptive' is much nearer the mark. The following is a case of poltergeistic activity and possibly possession. In it, the possession of the house seems to have been merely the by-product of the 'possession' of a person.

This story concerns the Dunne family from the north of England who came over when the husband got a job as an electrician in Shorts, in Belfast. They bought a newish semi-detached house in Sydenham, which was handy to his work.

Mrs Dunne spent most of her time at home with her two daughters. She was often alone there, for her husband worked long hours. After a while she began feeling uncomfortable sensations when she was in the house. Over time these crystallised into the distinct feeling that she was being watched.

'It is as though someone is standing behind me,' she told me. 'But when I turn around, there is no one there.'

She also noticed that small items in cupboards and on shelves were being moved about, and not by her! She decided to say nothing to the rest of the family, but the strain began to tell. As the weeks passed, her sensation of being followed as she did her chores became stronger, and on a couple of occasions she had the sensation of someone speaking to her. At night, she believed there to be someone standing by the bed. Lights in various rooms began to behave strangely. Was the wiring defective? Her husband checked it. The wiring seemed sound. What was going on? Mrs Dunne decided to seek help, and a friend who had heard me lecture suggested that she get in touch.

We met one autumn evening at her house, along with a fellow member of the Society for Psychical Research, who came along to monitor our conversation. In the meantime there seemed to have been no new developments, no picking up of the pace. Although on looking back there was perhaps one important change. Mrs Dunne was now emphatic that she could tell when the thing came into the room.

'I feel cold,' she said. 'And there's a sort of shadow in the corner of the room where she stands.'

I noticed that the entity had acquired a gender.

Some minutes later, in the middle of our conversation, Mrs Dunne indicated that the entity was present. Her whole demeanour changed. She immediately became unsettled. Nothing altered for the rest of us, but Mrs D was clearly in difficulty. I felt her hands, they were ice cold, in spite of the warmth of the room.

'I think it feels you could help,' she reported. 'I keep thinking of the name Isa,' she said suddenly. 'I don't know why, I've always thought of "her" as Millie.'

My colleague looked at me.

'We know an Isa,' she said. 'Maybe she could help?'

I nodded, though I knew little of spiritualism. We told Mrs Dunne that we would speak to our clairvoyant friend Isa, and see if she thought there was anything she could do.

In the meantime we found out what we could about the house and its location. We discovered that the street had been built on land belonging to someone connected with the shipyard. His house had been pulled down and the grounds sold for development in the 1930s. Mr Dunne made his own enquiries, and came up with the same story, adding that the man was called Stuart or Stewart, and that he had had a daughter.

We spoke to Mr Dunne over a cup of coffee. He was concerned for his wife, of course, but particularly mystified by the maverick electrics. He had been round the circuit several times, but had been unable to isolate the problem. Indeed, his considered view was that there was no problem, no physical problem anyway. But the electrics continued to be erratic. The lights flashed on and off in the children's room, frightening them out of their wits.

Everyone agreed that something needed to be done. I got hold of Isa.

'What would you like me to do?' she asked, obligingly. We discussed the problem.

'Mmm. I think we should sit in circle [hold a seance] and see what comes through,' she ventured. The Dunnes were agreeable. A meeting was arranged.

By the date of the meeting the presence in the house had become more intrusive still. It had by this point apparently assumed a vague physical form. It seemed to be making a determined journey towards three dimensionality. Mrs Dunne described it as 'a small, slight figure in a black dress'. She remained open to its attempts at contact.

'I feel so sorry for her,' she would say. 'I know she is unhappy and afraid.'

A mediumistic circle was duly convened. I have no clairvoyant ability, but anyway sat in as a guest. Isa led. She was a very capable medium, who had worked with many so-called 'rescue circles', trying to help discarnate personalities find their way. On this occasion, she contacted a young woman called Mildred or Millie, who professed herself to be the daughter of the owner of the house that once stood here. Gradually, over three meetings, we built up the stark picture of a bullying father, and a frightened daughter so terrified of her father that she wished him dead. The father did die, apparently of a stroke, and Mildred was overcome with guilt, and the feeling that she had caused his death. To this was added a fear of encountering the old tyrant, if such he was, in the afterlife.

Mildred died in the flu epidemic that followed the First World War, but instead of 'progressing', she clung to the place she knew, and became what Isa called 'earthbound'. Then, of course, the house was destroyed, and new streets went up. Mildred endeavoured to attach herself to people who might be able to help, and that is how Mrs Dunne became involved, as perhaps others had been before her.

It was the most unusual case of possession I had ever heard. It was disconcerting too. Disconcerting to think that fear of another could last beyond the grave. And professionally disconcerting in that, for all my receptivity, I had not been able to discern 'Mildred's' presence. The meetings seemed to help. The disturbances in the house grew less. The electrics worked better. Mrs Dunne seemed more relaxed.

The Dunnes moved back to England not long afterwards. Shortly before they left, Isa and I called to say goodbye. Mrs D had something to tell us.

'I don't know whether there is anything in this,' she said, 'but when I was in the kitchen the other afternoon, I felt someone beside me, and a light touch on my arm. I felt a great sense of peace,' she said slowly. 'I knew she had come to say goodbye.' I do hope that that wasn't wishful thinking.

Poltergeist

The term poltergeist means 'noisy, boisterous spirit', and poltergeistic activity is one of the most commonly encountered paranormal manifestations. It can include the lifting, throwing, and smashing of objects, floods of water, and occasionally slapping or pushing and minor physical injury, for it is one of the few paranormal events that can cause actual bodily harm. It can also emerge along with fire raising and the appearance of apparitions.

When we investigate poltergeistic activity, or Recurrent Spontaneous Psychokinesis (RSPK), to give it its technical name, we typically look for the involvement of a child or young person at the age of puberty or adolescence. By its very nature RSPK is open to fraud, but in many cases the reports of it are multiply witnessed, and would seem to have a genuine basis.

In over forty years I have had more than a hundred poltergeistic cases reported to me by respectable witnesses. Poltergeistic activity is often startling and apparently capricious. It can end as abruptly as it begins. Sometimes it will repeat in the same place at a later time, with the same, or sometimes different witnesses.

Ireland has a long and interesting history of this phenomenon. Some cases have achieved a measure of notoriety, including the Cooneen Ghost, in County Fermanagh, which is alleged to have so terrified the family it victimised, that they emigrated to the USA to escape it! One member of the family, Maggie, the eldest daughter, seemed to be the centre of the attention. There were many witnesses to its tirades, including a number of clergy, and at one point the 'energy' caused seventeen pages to be torn bodily from a large family bible.

Another case of note, also from Fermanagh, interestingly enough, was the Derrygonnelly case of 1911, in which the energy took part in an astonishing proxy conversation with witnesses, rapping 'yes', or 'no' to questions, and counting out numbers.

The following examples both took place in my presence, one in a farmhouse outside Coalisland in County Tyrone, and one in an old house in County Down. In the latter instance, I saw a lit candle move from one end of the mantelpiece to the other, in a smooth gliding motion which left the flame steady, and to all appearances blissfully undisturbed. The deliberateness of the movement implied conscious direction, i.e. poltergeistic involvement. This happened at intervals over a period of three years, then ceased entirely. There were a number of witnesses.

The Tyrone poltergeist was first experienced by the farmer and his family, and as a result I was asked to investigate. At regular intervals, the family's large scrubbed, wooden kitchen table would move of its own volition by rocking back and forth on its four sturdy legs. The farmer described this as 'dancing', and the word was very apt. The dance occurred at the most disruptive time possible – at around 6.30 pm of an evening when the family were seated around the table having tea. Hardly surprising that when the dance began the family with one accord would quit the table and rush into the hall, to watch it from a safe distance!

The farmer, a sensible and logical man, found it very hard to come to terms with what he was seeing, and told my fellow researcher and I so in no uncertain terms. For all his fighting talk, however, we noted with a smile that when the performance began he was always the first to evacuate the kitchen and view it from halfway up the stairs!

Once the table has ceased to gyrate, we examined it for any sign of a hoax and found none. There were no wires or pulling devices; I crawled under the table and met with no resistance of any kind. The floor was stable and even. I found no evidence of any kind of tampering at all. After a short while, some weeks or

*'He was always the first to evacuate the kitchen,
and view it from the stairs...'*

so, the table hung up its dancing shoes, and never ceili'd again.
It was baffling. Quite baffling. My only hunch was that the
movements might have had something to do with a young man
of limited mental capacity, who was invariably present when the
table danced. I wondered if he was the unconscious 'lord of the
dance', the supplier or conduit of the energy that made the table
quiver, but I had no means of proving it either way.

Another case worth mentioning in passing also concerned an
elderly farmer (why the farming community was picked on in
this way I have no idea!), who lived in a remote area of Fermanagh.
He complained constantly to his neighbours that 'he was
tormented by a sack of meal'. It appeared that at bedtime he
would be followed up the stairs by a sack of meal that he kept at
the back door to feed the hens. Once at the top of the stairs, he
insisted that he was invisibly lifted and dumped upside down in
the sack! As a strict teetotaller, an active Presbyterian, and an
Orangeman to boot, this farmer was a bulwark of the local
community, and so made a most interesting witness. When the
story got to me, which these things invariably did, it had acquired

an added twist. Early one evening his near neighbour, who had occasion to drive past the back door of the farm, saw across the yard what he took to be his farming friend being followed by a dark, 'dumpy' kind of figure, that in his eyes looked suspiciously like a sack of meal...

The Jumping Picture

The following small incident took place in the early hours of a July morning in 1988, in the home of a well-known surgeon and his family. The incident fits into no neat category, and I still find it hard to classify. It is not straightforwardly poltergeistic. It did not appear to be related to any other event, although over the years there had been other odd occurrences in the house – unknown footfalls on the stairs, crockery moving in the kitchen, a door in the hall that would open of its own accord, and a sense, shared by all the family, of there being a 'presence' in the building.

This particular incident occurred early one Saturday morning in summer, before the Bs, a family of three, were up. An unusual noise was heard in the large sitting room below the main bedroom, so the husband went to investigate. When he got down he discovered that a large picture had 'jumped' off the wall over the hearth, without damaging or touching any other item or ornament, and finished up on the hearth rug, with the picture cord intact. The picture, an African watercolour given to him in Zimbabwe, was lying face down on the rug, undamaged except for one small chip. Nothing else was broken, although to reach the floor the picture had had to 'jump' over a fairly ample marble mantelshelf, well stocked with Dresden figurines. None of these was even touched; and there were no signs of a break in.

Being a resourceful man, Mr B photographed the scene, before setting the picture upright on a chair. I saw this picture later the same day when Mrs B asked me to call round.

I was baffled as to how the picture had 'leapt' over the

assembled ornaments and done no damage. Oddly enough, I would have expected it to have fallen face upwards, bearing in mind the weight involved, but no, it had fallen face down. It was then that I heard about other events in the house, including the removal of a collection of heavy dinner plates from the table to a large Welsh dresser. The lady of the house had found this later the same evening when she had gone into the kitchen to tidy up before bed.

'I knew I hadn't touched them,' she said. 'That job was still there to be done.'

'You've always felt a presence in the house?' I asked. She grinned ruefully.

'Its not normally as helpful,' she pointed out, giving me the feeling that this was 'help' she might have been happier without!

I gazed outside. The house, which still had its original stable yard and outbuildings, made for a very attractive home. It had an interesting history. Not far from the edge of Lisburn, it had in its time been a coaching inn on the Dublin 'run', a post office, and small shop. There was also a local belief that during the early twentieth century, a murder had been committed there.

Its previous owner, an elderly lady, lived only a half mile away, and she was reputed to be quite ill. A vague thought linked the event of the picture 'falling' with the imminence of a death, but on reflection I thought that this was stretching things a bit. A falling picture is an almost archetypal portent of death. But this was rather different, I felt.

Nothing like it happened again, the elderly lady recovered, and there were no other untoward events in the house, where, incidentally, the Bs still live. Mind you, there is still that indefinable presence that appears to bother nobody, and the door in the hall still swings mysteriously open.

Counting the Spoons

This episode took place early on in my investigative career, and I have to confess that, in all my years of paranormal inquiry, I can think of no account that gives me more pleasure than this one. It is the story of a holiday haunting, and it is a curious fact that many people who have never had a brush with the paranormal before, will have one when on holiday. The theory is that the mind is relatively relaxed when on holiday, and may therefore register events which do not normally get a look in because of pressure from everyday matters.

This is an account of what happened to two families sharing a holiday home near Portnoo, in County Donegal. One of those families was my own. Both had small children; and while my husband Stanley and I had some experience of the paranormal, our friends Bob and Marion had no such experience to draw on, and no particular interest in the subject besides.

Now, with the notable exception of the children, we were all to bear witness to some very strange goings on indeed. The first thing we discovered, quite early on, was that our holiday home, a nineteenth century shooting lodge, had something of a reputation locally, although whenever we attempted to explore this further we were met with hot denials! For example the local grocer's boy would carry our groceries willingly to the kitchen door, but no amount of coaxing would get him over the threshold, no matter how hot the day or how refreshing the lemonade I offered him might be. As the holiday progressed we began to understand his reluctance!

The other folk who gave the game away were the owners themselves, when they came to check the place at the holiday's end, and through their regular 'popping in', and then popping in again, 'just to check that everything was alright'.

I can understand their sensitivities. But I should also say that some house owners who have a brush with the paranormal positively revel in it, and I have been invited on many occasions to stay in homes that have an unseen guest, so that I may attempt to solve the mystery for the owners. Indeed, if the 'ghost' does not oblige by manifesting, the owners feel positively disgruntled!

Not everyone is enthusiastic of course. I have in mind the lady owner of a small guesthouse in mid-Ulster, who quite blatantly attempted to bribe me into keeping a discreet silence about a little old lady who flitted about the hall from time to time, then disappeared through a wall! I went along with this, but salved my conscience by attaching great weight to the fact that the aforesaid lady had never disappeared through a wall in my presence, but chosen instead to leave sedately by the door!

But to return to the story of the spoons. For the first couple of days we found nothing amiss. Our holiday home was very pleasant, with spacious accommodation and a well-equipped kitchen. On the fourth night, however, things got out of hand. The children had been in bed for some hours, when we adults decided to call it a night, and tumbled into our beds secure in the knowledge that we had left the place neat and tidy for a good start in the morning.

Suddenly, the most incredible racket commenced in the kitchen. We could hear the crockery on the big dresser being clattered about, and most bizarre of all, the noise of the turf-fuelled oven being vigorously raked.

Having myself some forty minutes earlier put all the dishes away on the dresser, and carefully raked the ashes, I was quite mystified. My husband and I stole into the hall to find our pyjama-clad friends listening intently at the green baize door that led to the kitchen, further down the hall.

'I thought you'd finished for the night,' hissed Marion. 'I would have helped!'

She had left me washing up in the kitchen, and for all she knew I had not gone to bed.

I shook my head.

'I thought it was you,' I hissed back.

By now the noises had stopped, and all was as quiet as the grave, if you'll excuse the expression. I realised that we were talking in whispers, and had no idea why. The two men metaphorically squared their shoulders then marched down to the kitchen door and flung it open.

The kitchen was in darkness, and was ominously quiet. When we switched on the lights there was no one there, save ourselves. Every dish was neatly stacked on the dresser, and the range was as I left it, except that the smoking turf now gave off a comforting red glow. For good measure Bob checked the back door. It was locked. Nothing was amiss in the pantry, and the tiny maid's room off the kitchen was empty.

Realising that this was not a good time to hold a council of war, we crept back to our respective bedrooms, glad that the children had not woken and added to the confusion.

Next morning we decided, rather unrealistically, that the noises had come from outside. I was nagged by the feeling that I had somehow triggered the disturbance. My husband was less diplomatic.

'I thought you might have switched off while we were on holiday,' he rasped. This dig did not merit a reply, I thought resentfully, indignant at being given the blame for the entire episode. I consoled myself with the thought that it was probably a one off, maybe an anniversary manifestation. I couldn't have been more wrong.

Night after night, the kitchen was swept clean and the dishes thumped back on the dresser. The fire too, got regular attention, and we could hear the sound of chairs being arranged around the kitchen table. Time after time, singly and together, we padded down to the kitchen, only to find it dark and empty. Curiously enough, after these interruptions the clearing up never restarted. Once a night was, mercifully, quite enough!

Other things happened too. When I went to clean out the

fire in the living room with a bucket and small shovel, in the time it took for me to empty the ashes, the shovel would have migrated to the dining room, leaving the sticks for the fire unmolested.

Then began the episode with the spoons. A serving hatch linked the dining room and the kitchen. Attached to it was a shelf that one filled up on the kitchen side, then revolved round to the dining room side, where one's fellow server would unload it to lay up the meal. There was just one snag. No matter how meticulously you counted the cutlery out onto the revolving shelf in the kitchen, by the time it got to the dining room there was always some item missing – a couple of spoons maybe, or a knife and two forks. We got tired of blaming each other for miscounting the cutlery, but more wearing still, when we returned the cutlery to the kitchen the number of items was always irritatingly correct.

As you will appreciate, the atmosphere in the house was beginning to become decidedly fraught! Marion for example refused to stay alone in the house, and when we went out, she would switch on all the lights, open the windows and walk about with her head permanently turned over her shoulder.

In spite of all the stresses and strains our noisy friend was causing, we decided to play it cool and say nothing to our host, who by now was calling regularly 'just to make sure that everything was alright'. When asked we always looked cheery and replied in the affirmative, which I suspect he found rather baffling.

And so our holiday ended. It had had its moments, but the friendship between our families survived. We saw no 'ghosts'. We heard no voices, and outside the kitchen/ dining area, everything was completely normal. I wondered if we had come across a former servant at her chores, maybe the maid who had occupied the little room off the kitchen, in the days when the house was in its prime?

The final denouement came on the last day of our holiday, when the owner came to collect the keys and sign the inventory.

'You had a nice time?' he managed a smile.

'Yes, thank you,' we chorused, and then watched in fascinated silence as, quite oblivious of our presence, he crossed the room to the cutlery drawer and began to count the spoons.

The Little Lad of Tempo

This story of murder and disturbance will strike a chord of horrified compassion in the reader for the 'little lad' so casually done to death, and so shamefully treated after it. Its paranormal content is poltergeistic, the appearance and disappearance of small, spontaneous fires in the house being a clear signal of poltergeistic involvement.

The house itself was decidedly chilly, but I think this had more to do with the weather than 'the ether'. Stately homes are a little like fridges in winter. In the days before central heating they tended to have a little core of warmth, usually round the range, but once you moved beyond that you were lost. Lady Langham very kindly saw me in a huge reception room containing a three bar electric heater, one bar of which was switched on. Even her small dog wore a pullover, in a rather fetching Fairisle pattern, and sat on the end of the sofa nearest the 'fire', curling his lip in the most threatening manner should anyone come close enough to unseat him.

During the icy winter of 1971, I was sitting by the fire in Tempo Manor, County Fermanagh, enjoying the company of the late Lady Rosamond Langham, the then chatelaine of this beautiful manor house. I was glad to be close to the fire, or rather heater, for the house was freezing. Lady Langham, however, seemed quite oblivious to the cold. We talked about poetry. Then the conversation turned to another subject of mutual interest, the paranormal, and she told me the strange, centuries old story of 'the little lad', as it had come down to her within the family.

Before their dispossession in the seventeenth century, the local lords were the Maguires, and they bred fine quality racehorses. When the local gentry organised races between their animals, the Maguire horses regularly won, which was a source of great pride and prestige to the family. Each horse was accompanied to the meet by a stable boy, who stayed overnight with the horse in its loosebox, to guard against any skulduggery. On the eve of one of these meetings, held at Tempo, one of the leading Maguires of the day was scared that a fine horse owned by a rival might trounce his best horses, so he set about plotting how to 'nobble' the visiting horse.

The method he settled on was to 'persuade' the young and vulnerable stable boy to sabotage his horse. When the favoured horse arrived at Tempo, this particular Maguire attempted to bribe his boy to do the horse a mischief. The little lad refused, whereon his host lost his temper and killed him. He did so with a sense of impunity. The boy was a nobody, probably from a poor serving family, if he had any family at all. He would not be missed. The flagstone outside the loose box was then hurriedly dug up and the body concealed beneath it, and the story put about that the boy (whose name, alas, has not come down to us) had run away.

During the nineteenth century, another owner of the manor, one of the Langham family, curious to know if there was any truth in this by now well known story, had the stone dug up. Beneath the flag, he found the skeletal remains of a boy, just as had been conjectured. The owner then had the remains brought into the house and exhibited in his private museum, in the company of various botanical specimens and monkey bones, brought home from abroad.

This was not a good idea. The household began to experience a series of strange disturbances. The family dogs refused to go anywhere near the museum. Small spontaneous fires erupted in various parts of the house. The building's 'atmosphere' changed. Its pleasantness gave way to a feeling that all was not well.

Finally, the Langhams came to the conclusion that the bones of the murdered boy were the source of their misfortune. It was decided to remove the remains. But the reburial was botched.

'Beneath the flag, he found the skeletal remains of a boy...'

Instead of interring them in a cemetery, the Langhams had the troublesome skeleton covertly buried in the shrubbery of the house, at a place known only to senior members of the family. However, if the Langhams thought that this would be the end of the matter, they were mistaken. The loosebox continued to be a place of dread. Animals housed in it would be discovered drenched in sweat and terrified out of their lives. In quite recent times a group of pedigree calves housed in the box overnight were discovered in this condition. One of the calves had attempted to jump through a glass window and gashed himself fatally. After this only baled hay or implements were kept in the box.

My hostess sighed.

'And so it has remained till this day,' she said. 'If you'd like to come with me I'll show you the stables.'

So off we went. We came on an attractive range of outhouses surrounding a cobbled yard, with flagstones outside the doors of the looseboxes. The notorious box looked ordinary enough as I stepped inside to look around. Save for some baled hay, there was nothing untoward about it. The flagstone outside seemed ordinary enough too. But when I stepped on it a curious chill seemed rise from it, and it seemed faintly moist. It was highly disconcerting. I stepped off it hurriedly, trying to rationalise the sense of unease the stone gave me.

In some disarray I recognised a feeling I had experienced on only one or two occasions – a clear and eerie sense of linkage with the past, and a murdered child whose life had been brutally cut short, a sharp and most distressful pang of contact with the little lad from Tempo.

Piper s Hill

In the older part of Lisburn, there is a narrow lane known as Piper's Hill, which runs from the town centre down to the site of the old Brown Linen Hall. Nowadays the lane is home to the town's health centre, but until recent times it contained an extraordinary row of two-storied weavers' cottages, each of which had a large cellar beneath the living rooms which once contained a loom. The houses had no back doors. They were built into rock at the rear, so that everyone who came and went did so through the half door that opened onto the Hill. Both our accounts from Piper's Hill, one apparitional and one poltergeistic, come from these cottages.

The first concerns number twelve. Its occupier, Mr H.D., was looking for a discount on his rates, claiming that 'everyone knew he had a fella who tramped up and down his stairs every night, and put him away in the head'. The authorities duly considered his complaint, and refused his application.

A newspaper editor of my acquaintance suggested I go and see him. I did so gladly. I felt a certain amount of admiration for this plucky old gentleman fighting against officialdom, and was intrigued by his claims, so I decided to call with a view to interviewing him for a programme I was preparing for Radio Ulster.

The recording went like a dream. H.D. proved a 'natural'. When we'd finished I asked if he knew of anyone who could confirm his story? Yes, he answered, his next door neighbour, an old lady in her eighties.

'She'll tell you,' he insisted. 'Sure aren't the stairs on her side of the wall? She must have heard his tramping.'

So I went next door, where I received a typical Ulster welcome. The lady asked me in and told me to sit down while she wetted the tea. Our conversation was most revealing. Not only did Miss N.B. entirely trash her neighbour's complaint, she also gave me quite an earful on the subject of 'the old rogue's' drinking and tall stories. His credibility as a witness soon lay in tatters.

'He never heard nathin,' she declared, plunging the knife in once more, 'his wits are addled.' Sadder but wiser, I packed up my tape recorder and got ready to go. As I made for the door, she said, 'If he saw the woman I seen in the kitchen, he'd have something to shout about.' That stopped me in my tracks.

'A woman, what woman?'

Every night apparently, a woman with folded arms stood silently at the old lady's kitchen fire. She wore a long grey dress, over which she had a big white apron, and a cap of similar material. It reminded me of a description of a female spinner or weaver that I had heard before from elsewhere.

It seemed that she would stand beside the fire, then after a while withdraw behind the curtain that led to the small scullery. If one followed her one would find nothing. Night after night she would come and keep the old lady company. It had been like this for months, but alas, there were no other witnesses. I asked N.B. what she made of it all.

The old lady sniffed.

'She says nathin' t' me and I say nathin t' her,' she added curtly.

'So she doesn't annoy you?' I queried.

She shook her head. 'I never mind her,' she said. 'Sure it must have been her kitchen afore it was mine.' A piece of logic I had not bargained on! The old lady seemed completely unfazed. Indeed I sensed that a certain sense of 'sisterhood' had grown up between them.

Not all the Piper's Hill presences were so companionable. The MacC family lived in number thirteen. There were five of them, two adults and three children of varying ages, none of them adolescent. One morning, Mrs MacC thought she heard feet walking about in the bedroom. Thinking that one of the children might have sneaked back from school, she went to the foot of the stairs and called out. Receiving no reply, she began to climb the stairs. At that moment, the sound of feet ceased. She described them to me as 'a heavy foot and a light foot'. Her clergyman later suggested that the noise might have been rats. She replied, 'If its rats Father, thon wears quare heavy boots' – a remark a little reminiscent of Mr H.D.'s complaint.

A number of neighbours also heard the footfalls, and over the following weeks the intensity of the disturbances increased. Furniture moved. Bedcovers were tossed around. Mr MacC was bodily thrown out of bed. A heavy mirror was hurled from a window. During all this the terrified family slept huddled together in the downstairs room with all the lights on, night and day. The press became interested, so the family had journalists and inquisitive members of the public, as well as a poltergeist to contend with. Neighbours, clergymen and the police took to calling at all hours of the day and night in a futile attempt to reassure the family. But the disturbances continued, so the clergy advised the parents to move out, if only temporarily, to ensure their safety.

The family stayed put. But the stress became so unbearable that Mrs MacC suffered a breakdown and had to be hospitalised for several weeks. Mr H.D. was, naturally enough, extremely concerned. He also saw it as confirmation of his own story.

'Didn't I tell ye?' he said over and over again.

It was at this point that I became involved. I was asked by a friend of Mrs MacC's to go and talk to her, in case I could help. I listened to her story, but very much regret to say that I was unable to do any good. I had arrived too late. After I had heard everything, I asked her if she had any idea who or what had done these things? She gave me the most plaintive look:

'It's the Noonday Devil,' she said. 'Like it says in the Bible, the Noonday Devil seeking what it can destroy.'

Odours Pleasant & Unpleasant

There must be very few of us who don't have in our memories a smell that recalls childhood, or evokes some particular person. For me it is the smell of tar, which I associate with a trip to the local gasworks as a child, where I was taken to cure my whooping cough. Another wonderfully nostalgic smell for me is lily-of-the-valley, my mother's favourite perfume. Even though the associations are over fifty years old, these smells still waft me back to childhood.

Odours pleasant and unpleasant are an integral part of the paranormal experience. Researchers, rather grandly, know them as 'olfactory manifestations'. Though they are often mixed up with other phenomena, they can appear on their own, and are an interesting, if somewhat disconcerting, paranormal manifestation in their own right.

One afternoon about fifteen years ago I was contacted by a mother who had just lost her only child to a terminal illness. Her daughter Mary was just twelve years old.

During the child's hospitalisation, when everything got too much for her, the lady had taken to sitting in the child's bedroom on her own. She had found this comforting. After Mary died she could not bear to turn the room to other uses, and so kept it much as it had been when her little daughter was alive.

Then she began to notice that whenever she sat in the room she could detect almost at once the strong, sweet smell of violets, her favourite flower, though there was no material reason why the smell should be present. She found this very consoling.

'It felt as though Mary was very close to me. This lasted for some weeks, and sometimes, even yet, I think I can smell the perfume.'

I explained how smells were often tied up with the recollection of a memory, and that in due course, when it had served its purpose, the smell from which she had derived such comfort would disappear.

This reminded me of my friend Jean, a teacher, who some years before had lost her mother after a crippling illness. She too had experienced an 'odour' at the time of death, and what is more unusual, so had her sister, who lived many miles away from them both. Jean lived in Belfast, and she became aware of the smell while standing on the steps of Church House, in Fisherwick Place in Belfast, during the last days of her mother's illness.

'The clock above struck noon, and suddenly I became aware of the overpowering smell of funeral lilies – or some pungent hothouse bloom. I turned to my companion and said, "I must go home. My mother has just died."

She immediately returned home. As she opened the front door the telephone was ringing. It was her father to tell her that about ten minutes before, her mother had died quite unexpectedly.

'I was in no doubt as to what had happened,' she said. 'I just knew.'

On the same morning at about noon, some six hundred miles away, her sister was standing talking to her neighbour across the garden wall when she suddenly smelt the unmistakable smell of damp earth being turned. She excused herself to her friend by saying, 'I'm sorry, I must make a phone call, my mother has just died!'

Like her sister, she knew immediately that she had been sent a message. In that fleeting moment, the minds of the three women had meshed. For the dying woman, it was her final goodbye to her two much loved daughters, and for them, the knowledge that, even at the last, they had been in their mother's thoughts.

Not all smell related incidents are this consoling, alas. In the latter part of 1986 Mrs MacB, a very upright Methodist lady from Lisburn, was coming home from Moira one evening. She was due to meet her husband in the town centre, and, as she was a little late, she took a short cut, in the hope that it might get her there in time. Her way led up the narrow lane known as Piper's Hill. According to local legend, this atmospheric old laneway marks the path taken by condemned men on their way to the gallows in the seventeenth or eighteenth century.

Mrs MacB was not thinking on this as she hurried up the hill to her rendezvous. Halfway up, opposite the site of the old weavers' cottages where the health centre now stands she suddenly felt herself in the middle of a most appalling stench. The smell was so powerful that it seemed as if a thick miasma had formed about her, and she lost sight of the top of the hill, though it was only yards distant.

'I felt I was choking,' she said with a shudder. 'I could go neither backward or forward. And I was conscious of something terrible having happened.'

She fainted and fell to the ground, then woke to find a passer-by alongside her, trying to bring her round. All the while her anxious husband waited in the square, unaware of his wife's mishap.

Some weeks afterwards, having got over her fright, Mrs MacB phoned me and asked me to call. She didn't need to tell me too much about the lane. I knew it well. This was not the first time that there had been untoward events on 'the Hill' as it was known, and few of them had been pleasant. (See *Piper's Hill*) Mrs MacB's experience was one of a considerable number. Nothing I heard about 'the Hill' completely surprised me. It had a kind of mordant air, even in the daytime. I am told that such an 'atmosphere' can be felt by people visiting Auschwitz.

But what about Mrs MacB? Somehow, her mind has inadvertently laid itself open to the conditions that were present on the hill. These phenomena are usually extremely elusive, but somehow she had connected with them. The only other thing that I could think to say to her was that the experience was unlikely to be repeated.

'You can bank on that,' she said with gusto. 'It'll be a while before I take that short cut again.'

And one could hardly blame her.

The Phantom Hitchhiker

This phenomenon is known all over the world and in particular in the United States. It is, as one writer has affirmed, a perennially repeated narrative, told and retold all over the globe. The hitchhiker that appeared in Ulster over twenty odd years ago is, in as far as I can ascertain, the only 'phantom hitchhiker' known from the province.

The reactions of the drivers who saw her varied from a desire to report the incident, to a strong and very understandable impulse to simply drive home and try and forget the whole thing. The drivers were also almost always male, and they came from various walks of life – a prison warder, lorry drivers, ordinary motorists, etc. Several sightings were reported to me through third parties. Other witnesses came to see me at home.

They all told roughly the same story. The spot where it happened was always the same. They always described their passenger in similar terms, giving me identical details of appearance, dress and hair. They all reported that the seat beside them had depressed as the person got in, and that they 'felt' the person beside them. In one instance the driver, aware of a faulty lock on the passenger door, had leaned across to make sure it was shut, and unequivocally vouched that there was someone sitting beside him in the passenger seat.

Their story was quite simple. In the clearest version given to me the motorist was driving out of Belfast towards Hillsborough on the M1 when suddenly his headlights picked up a lone figure standing on the hard shoulder. It was a young woman in her early twenties, wearing a winter coat, apparently looking for a lift. She had no bag, and thought it was a cold night, no mits or gloves. The motorist, a warder at the Crumlin Road jail in Belfast, drew over and opened his passenger door. A father himself, he was uneasy at such a young girl being on her own on that lonely stretch of road.

The girl got in, and he leaned over her to check that the door, surprised that she had not spoken to him. He asked her where she was going, but received no reply, so he wisely left her to herself for some moments. Within about five hundred yards, he suddenly felt an icy chill in the car. Turning sideways a little, he saw to his horror that his passenger had vanished! Instinctively, he braked hard bringing the car screeching to a halt, and then stumbled outside. Fortunately there was no vehicle behind him. There was no one anywhere. The road lay still in the moonlight, and there was no one in sight, either up or down the highway. Collecting himself, he checked the passenger door, but there was no way it could have swung open and closed itself again. There was no way the girl could have got out.

When he was calm enough to be able to drive again, the man got back into the car and headed for the police station in his home town of Banbridge. He had no idea what he was going to say, but he had to tell someone what had happened. The upshot of it all was that he ended up on my doorstep, and I listened to his tale.

He got extremely emotional as he told it.

'You don't believe me,' he exclaimed. 'I wasn't drinking or dreaming. That girl got into my car.'

'I know,' I said gently. 'I know because you are not the only one.'

None of us knew much about 'phantom hitchhikers' then. Now I know that the sequence of events is very similar whether the hitchhiker is given a lift in Belfast or Barcelona, and that the circumstances surrounding the Ulster hitching make it fairly well a classic of its kind. I also know that these tales have a historical pedigree. Accounts of 'vanishing travellers' occur through the centuries, and while the vehicles have changed over time, the basic sequence of events has not.

Sometimes local tradition will hang the story of a fatal accident on them, for it is in our nature to find logical conclusions, and to have no loose ends. This is what happened in the Ulster case, and I can make no comment as I genuinely don't know how to explain this. The people involved were all sincere people. They knew what they had been involved in, and now sought some explanation.

I tried to help. One possibility, thinking of the swiftness of the separation of body and consciousness often involved in a road death, is that the victim does not realise that she is clinically dead, but will materialise in her discarnate body until she runs out of 'energy'. That at least makes a kind of crazy sense to those of us who believe in life after death.

In this case, on Christmas Eve, about a year before the phantom hitchhiker was seen, a young girl was fatally injured on the motorway by a drunken driver coming down the wrong side of the carriageway and colliding with her car, killing her instantly. When the emergency services took her body away, they left behind her gloves and handbag. It is worth mentioning again that all the drivers who saw her agreed that whoever they saw had neither gloves nor bag, only a coat.

The theories that have been produced to explain the phenomenon range from the idea that the 'hitchhiker' is a messenger delivering a warning of tragedy (not so in this case), to the claim that the drivers have experienced some kind of collective hallucination.

Over a period of two years the hitchhiker was seen half a dozen times, always in the same area, only once being reported on the other side of the carriageway. But I have heard nothing more for many years now. Come Christmas, if one is sensitive and sympathetic, one thinks of a young girl, lost and alone on a strange road at night. What would her first thought be? I would think it would be to try and get back home ...

The Coming of the Light

There is a particular feeling of blessedness about Christmas Eve, and as a small child I lived in the country in an age when there always seemed to be a sprinkle of snow on the ground and a bright moon shining, as we waited for the 'blessed morn,' to arrive.

When I was a child I shared a room with my younger sister. One Christmas Eve, when I was about six, I woke to find that our bedroom was filled with a light as bright as day, and I sleepily concluded that I had slept more peacefully than usual, and that Christmas morning had arrived. To my bafflement, the world outside the bedroom window was still dark. The light was confined to inside our room, where it lit up every nook and cranny, and picked out the bulging pillowcases stuffed with presents at the bottom of our beds.

Something, however, prevented me from exploring the goodies. Something told me it was not the time to explore.

I sat up in bed and waited, for what I had no idea.

All was still. Then I heard a noise, and to my astonishment, the drawers of a very old chest standing opposite my bed began to open very slowly, one after another. As there were seven drawers it took some time, but one by one they quietly slid open, and then equally noiselessly, slid shut, one after another. I can't remember feeling afraid, merely baffled by this phenomenon, and all the while, my sister slept soundly.

Gradually the light in the room faded, until it was night again and I could see a young moon sailing in the sky. I snuggled down into the blankets and must have fallen asleep once more. Then it was Christmas Day.

My second visitation occurred many years later, when I was grown and had a family of my own. It was a night in late autumn. I couldn't sleep and tossed restlessly into the small hours. I was grieving for my beloved mother, who that day had left us, and was torn between relief that her pain was over – and the anxiety of being left alone. Suddenly the bedroom seemed less dark, and I heard a voice saying, 'My peace I give onto you.' No more than that; and I drifted into a dreamless, healing slumber.

I recount these two incidents, not as examples of this or that, but simply because they are precious to me. However, they do, I suppose, make a point. They remind me that there are things that are paranormal, and fall within some natural law which we don't yet understand, and there are matters that derive from a higher authority. To try and explain the workings of this would be an impertinence. Yet in some curious way, I think they are linked. It is true that at present 'we see in a glass darkly'. But one day the light will come.

Select Bibliography

Fryer, Charles   *Geraldine Cummins: an Appreciation* (Pelegrin, 1990)
Green, Andrew   *Our Haunted Kingdom* (Wolfe, 1993)
Haynes, Renee   *The Society for Psychical Research 1888-1982*
                        (MacDonald, 1982)
Hough, Peter   *Supernatural Britain* (Piatkus, 1995)
Lysaght, Patricia   *The Banshee* (Glendale Press, 1989)
McKenzie, Andrew   *Hauntings and Apparitions* (Paladin, 1983)
Rogo, Dee Scott   *The Return from Silence* (Aquarian Press, 1989)
St.Clair, Sheila   *Psychic Phenomena in Ireland* (Mercier Press, 1972)
                        The Step on the Stair (Glendale Press, 1989)
                        Mysterious Ireland (Robert Hale, 1994)

Index

*Also available from
the White Row Press*

History

Arctic Ireland
*The extraordinary story of the
Great Frost and Forgotten Famine of 1740-41*

David Dickson

Pbk, 94 pp, illustrated, £4.95

On the last day of 1739, Ireland awoke to find itself in the grip of a mini Ice Age. The Lagan, the Boyne, the Liffey, the Shannon – and even Lough Neagh – had frozen, and houses could not be heated above freezing point. Many were enchanted by the novelty of it all. Carnivals, dances and sheep roastings were held on the ice.

But the euphoria proved fleeting. In its wake came an almost biblical ordeal by drought, flood, fire, famine and plague, that has few parallels in the recorded history of the island.

"for once the adjectives are fully justified. For the story of what happened over 250 years ago is truly extraordinary" *Sunday Times*

The Night of the Big Wind

Peter Carr

Pbk, 158 pp, illustrated, £4.95

The extraordinary story of one of Ireland's greatest natural disasters, the Big Wind of 1839, re-created from contemporary sources, and set in the context of the folk beliefs of the time. Includes an Ireland-wide A-Z of storm damage, and extended sections on the storm's meteorology and the role that religion and the supernatural played in attempting to explain it.

"An enthralling, gripping read" *Belfast News Letter*

"Written in a way which will appeal to everyone, whether an historian, or just an ordinary person who enjoys a good read" *Roe Valley Sentinel*

Literature

William Carleton: the Autobiography

William Carleton

Hbk & Pbk, 238 pp, £19.95 & £7.95

In the autumn of 1869, laden with accolades, but melancholic, written out, and ridden with the cancer that would shortly kill him, the novelist William Carleton turned to a subject as rich and difficult as any he had yet undertaken: himself.

The result was this fine – and alas unfinished – autobiography, a fresh vivid, vigorous work which covers the first twenty-eight years or so of his life. It takes him from a near idyllic childhood in the Clogher Valley to a bed of rags and straw shakedowns in Dirty Lane, Dublin, from which, equipped only with his genius and a powerful sense of destiny, the young Carleton went out upon the world.

Women are the Scourge of the Earth
Frances Molloy: Short Stories
Frances Molloy
Pbk, 107 pp, £5.95

"her writing strengthens the spirit and demonstrates how much explosive power can lie in the few, clear, telling words of the short story" *Honest Ulsterman*

Humour

Never!
Fascinating Facts about Ireland
Michael Smith
Pbk, 93 pp, illustrated, £3.95

Did you know... that the only Irishman to be offered the Papacy refused it? ...that an Irish ship discovered the ghostly remains of the *Marie Celeste*? ...or that the skull of an Irishman is the most sacred relic of the Ashanti tribe of west Africa?

All is now revealed in this illustrated collection of amusing, amazing and arcane facts relating to Ireland and the Irish.

"jam-packed with all sorts of scarcely believable, probably useless, but nonetheless fascinating gems of information" *Wicklow People*

Never Again!
More Fascinating Facts about Ireland
Michael Smith
Pbk, 93 pp, illustrated, £3.95

Did you know... that the Mounties were founded by an Irishman? ...that St. Valentine's bones are kept in a church in Dublin? ...that ChristopherColumbus was inspired to discover the New World by a story he heard in Galway?

Yet more is revealed in the sequel to the best-selling *Never!*

"this is not the deepest book you're likely to read this year, but it could well be the most absorbing" *Irish Post*

Available from bookshops or directly from the publishers. If ordering, please add £1 for postage & packaging. All prices quoted are in sterling.

To see our full range of titles, please visit our website:
www.whiterow.freeserve.co.uk